Nationalism and ∪

From Union to partition

Eilís Brennan
Belfast Education and Library Board

and

Sandra Gillespie
Bangor High School

Jonathan Bardon
Series Adviser

CAMBRIDGE
UNIVERSITY PRESS

For Elizabeth and Henry Brennan

Published by the Press Syndicate of the University of Cambridge
The Pitt Building, Trumpington Street, Cambridge CB2 1RP
40 West 20th Street, New York, NY 10011-4211, USA
10 Stamford Road, Oakleigh, Melbourne 3166, Australia

© Cambridge University Press 1996

First published 1996

Printed in Great Britain at the University Press, Cambridge

A catalogue record for this book is available from the British Library

Library of Congress cataloguing in publication data applied for

ISBN 0 521 46605 9

Designed and produced by Gecko Limited, Bicester, Oxon.

Picture research by Callie Kendall

Illustrations by Gerry Ball, Roger Jones, Martin Sanders, Neale Thomas, Robert Williams and Gecko Limited.

Front cover illustrations: Evicted, by Lady Butler, courtesy of the Department of Irish Folklore, University College Dublin. Stanford's London Atlas of Universal Geography, 1889, by permission of the Syndics of Cambridge University Library.

Notice to teachers

Many of the sources used in this textbook have been adapted or abridged from the original.

Acknowledgements

Every effort has been made to reach copyright holders; the publishers would be glad to hear from anyone whose rights they have unwittingly infringed.

4, Peter Newark's American Pictures; 5, Photographie Bulloz/Musée Carnavalet; 8, 9, 12, 13, 45l, National Gallery of Ireland; 10, Office of Public Works/courtesy of Blackstaff Press; 14, 16, 18, 34l, 39, 48, Mary Evans Picture Library; 19, courtesy of the Department of Irish Folklore, University College Dublin; 21, 29b, 30, 32, 33, 43, photograph reproduced with the kind permission of the Trustees of the Ulster Museum; 22, 35l, National Museum of Ireland; 26, 27, Mansell Collection; 28t, British Library, London/Bridgeman Art Library, London; 35r, 36, 45r, 46r; 47, 49, National Library of Ireland; 37, Hulton Deutsch Collection; 44l, Bob Thomas Sports Photography/Popperfoto; 44r, Christopher Hill Photographic; 46l, The Office of Public Works of Ireland/Kilmainham Gaol; 50r, Public Record Office of Northern Ireland; 50l, University College Dublin; 21, 29, 51l, 52b, 53l, 51r, 64, 66, 53r, 52t, 54, Punch Publications; 55, Trinity College Library, Dublin; 69, 70, 72, 67, 77, 76t, courtesy of Belfast City Council; 71, courtesy of The Office of Public Works of Ireland/painting by Thomas Ryan; 73, Crawford Art Gallery, Cork; 76b, Range/Bettmann/UPI; 78, 79t, Popperfoto; 79b, Pacemaker.

The publishers would like to thank Tony McAleavy, Carmel Gallagher and Christine Kinealy for their contributions to the writing of this book.

CONTENTS

Introduction:
The beginnings of nationalism and unionism

Section 1:
Two centuries of change

Section 2:
The development of unionism

Section 3:
A new century

Section 4:
The road to partition

The beginnings of nationalism and unionism

In the late 18th century the world was amazed by news of revolutions in America and France. Fuelled by a belief in democracy and equality, people in these and other countries rejected their governments and seized independence.

Which great international political changes in the 18th century formed the background to the 1798 rebellion?

In 1776 the settlers in America fought a war with Britain to gain their freedom and set themselves up as a new independent state – a republic. Inspired by the writings of Thomas Paine, they rejected the idea of kings, queens and nobility having special rights. Instead, they believed in a democratic system in which all people were equal and the country was run by an elected government.

Source A

Presenting the final draft of the Declaration of Independence in 1776. This painting by John Trumbull was completed in 1797.

In 1789, the people of France seized power from the King and the rich nobles, many of whom were executed. The French rebels believed in 'Liberty, Equality and Fraternity'. Instead of a few people having power and wealth, they wanted to set up a republic where all people were free and equal.

Inspired by events and ideas from abroad, there was an armed rebellion in Ireland in 1798. The rebels' aim was to secure freedom from England and to establish a fair and democratic Ireland for people of all religions. The failure of this rebellion resulted in the abolition of the Irish Parliament, and the Act of Union by which Ireland became part of the United Kingdom. Out of these events grew new forms of nationalism and unionism which were to shape the course of Irish history for the next 200 years.

Source B

Storming the Bastille, painted by Charles Thévenin in 1795.

The birth of nationalism

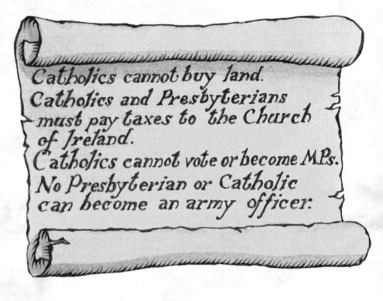

Catholics cannot buy land.
Catholics and Presbyterians must pay taxes to the Church of Ireland.
Catholics cannot vote or become MPs.
No Presbyterian or Catholic can become an army officer.

1 The first Irish nationalists were Protestants. Inspired by the Americans they demanded more power for the Dublin Parliament in the 1770s and 1780s. Ulster Presbyterians played a leading part in the early days of nationalism.

2 In the 18th century the Penal Laws discriminated against Catholics and Presbyterians in Ireland. As a result most land was owned by a small number of Protestant landlords. The laws were gradually abandoned after the 1770s.

3 A group called the United Irishmen tried to overthrow British rule by force in 1798. The rebels were supported by France. The British crushed the revolt of the United Irishmen. In 1800 the Dublin Parliament was abolished and there was a 'union' between Britain and Ireland.

4 In the first half of the 19th century Daniel O'Connell was the leading Irish nationalist. He believed that the use of violence was wrong. He had close connections with the Catholic Church. He helped Catholics to win the right to become MPs. He wanted a Parliament in Dublin.

5 Ireland was devastated by a great famine between 1845 and 1851. The crisis was triggered by a failure of the potato crop. Over a million people died and more fled the country. Many went to the USA.

6 Some nationalists looked back to the revolutionary ideas of the United Irishmen. Nationalists who believed in the use of force became known as Fenians from the late 1850s. There were failed attempts to organise armed rebellions in 1848 by Young Irelanders and 1867 by Fenians.

7 The Home Rule League was founded in 1873 to achieve a Parliament for Ireland through peaceful and legal means. The leader of this party was Isaac Butt.

1

Nationalism and unionism

Before 1800 many Protestants supported the idea of Irish independence. Some of them joined the United Irishmen to fight for an Irish Republic, yet during much of the 19th and 20th centuries most Protestants supported the link with Britain.

How did the Act of Union come about? And why did many Protestants change their attitude to the idea of Irish independence?

Grattan's Parliament

In the 18th century only about 25 per cent of the whole Irish population was Protestant but this minority dominated Irish politics. At this time Ireland had its own Parliament in Dublin and every member was a Protestant because Catholics were not allowed to become MPs.

Towards the end of the century many Irish people, including some MPs in the Dublin Parliament, began to question their link with Britain. They were deeply influenced by the revolution in America and the American Declaration of Independence of 1776. Nearly all of these Irish nationalists were Protestants.

In the 1770s and 1780s many Protestants formed an armed force, called the Irish Volunteers. In 1782 pressure from the Volunteers helped the Irish Parliament win the right to make laws of its own without reference to London. The leading politician at this time was Henry Grattan.

The Irish Volunteers in Belfast wanted Catholics to be treated equally and invited Catholic men to join their organisation. In 1789 the *Belfast News-letter* described the French Revolution as the 'greatest event' in human history.

Radical Belfast

When Grattan and his followers talked about an Irish nation, they were talking about a nation of wealthy Irish Protestant men. However, in Ulster, radical new ideas about equality were particularly popular with some Presbyterians who, like Catholics, were discriminated against. In the Belfast area there was a long tradition of independent thinking among Presbyterians and some of them wanted more reforms than Grattan and the Dublin Parliament.

Source A
Volunteers firing a salvo in College Green, Dublin, 1779, by Francis Wheatley.

The United Irishmen

In 1791, a radical organisation called the United Irishmen was founded in Belfast and Dublin. The United Irishmen were led by Protestants but they wanted Irish people of all faiths to unite in the struggle to create an independent Irish Republic which, like the American and French Republics, would not have a king. At the time, only wealthy men could vote; the United Irishmen wanted every man to have a vote. At first their methods were peaceful but later they decided to become a revolutionary organisation.

Theobald Wolfe Tone

Tone was a Dublin Protestant lawyer who sought to change the Irish Parliament. He was influenced by the French Revolution. He founded the United Irishmen to obtain rights for people of all religions. He sought help in France and America but was arrested during the 1798 rebellion and sentenced to death. Tone committed suicide in his cell. He is widely regarded as the first Irish Republican.

Source B
Theobald Wolfe Tone, 1763–1798.

Source C – The aims of Wolfe Tone

To break the connection with England, the never-failing source of our evils and to assert the independence of my country. These were my motives.

To unite the whole people of Ireland and to substitute the common name of Irishman in place of Protestant, Catholic or Dissenter – these were my means.

Wolfe Tone's Journal, 1791

The 1798 rebellion

In 1794 the government banned the United Irishmen because they feared their ideas and their links with the French Revolution. These Irishmen re-organised in Belfast as a secret revolutionary group, and pledged to set up a republican government for Ireland. A soldier called General Lake was given the task of crushing the United Irishmen in the north.

Source D

General Gerard Lake explained his attitude towards the United Irishmen of Belfast in 1797.

Nothing but terror will keep them in order. It is plain every act of sedition originates in this town.

With the help of informers, the leaders of the United Irishmen were arrested. Nearly fifty prisoners were executed, many of whom were Presbyterian ministers. This strong government action left the organisation of the United Irishmen in Ulster in ruins.

The British government tried to control the United Irishmen in other parts of Ireland. The revolutionaries were organised by a central committee in Dublin called the National Directory, led by a nobleman, Lord Edward Fitzgerald. In 1798 it decided to have a nationwide rebellion. The British government used the same robust methods which had been so successful in Ulster. Thousands of suspects were arrested and many of the rebels' weapons were captured.

In May 1798 the United Irishmen finally began their rebellion but they had a number of weaknesses:

- the organisation in Ulster was in ruins
- the national leadership had been arrested
- communications were poor
- there was a shortage of weapons.

In most places the rebels were easily defeated by government forces and many of the United Irishmen were captured and killed. It was only in Wexford that the rebels had any success. In the north the first event was an attack on Antrim town. This was led by Henry Joy McCracken, a Presbyterian businessman and one of the founders of the United Irishmen. The rebels were driven back and many were killed. After the disaster at Antrim the United Irishmen of County Down mobilised. They were defeated by government forces at Ballynahinch. Henry Joy McCracken and other leaders were captured and executed,

In October Wolfe Tone was captured on a ship which was part of a small French invasion force. The invasion failed; Tone was tried and sentenced to death but committed suicide in prison before he could be hanged. Although the 1798 rising failed, the United Irishmen had a great influence on later developments in Ireland.

Source E

A modern historian sums up the influence of Tone and the United Irishmen.

Wolfe Tone's United Irishmen became the model for later Irish nationalists. Their colour, green, became established as the national colour. Tone's grave at Bodenstown, County Kildare, is to the present day the site of annual pilgrimages and demonstrations by nationalist groups, determined, in his words, 'to break the connection with England'.

John O'Beirne Ranelagh, *A Short History of Ireland*, 1983

Source F

The Battle of Ballynahinch by Thomas Robinson.

The Act of Union 1800

The United Irishmen had a long-term impact on nationalism. In future years some nationalists found inspiration in the radical ideas of Tone and his friends. The rebellion of 1798 had a more immediate result: the British government decided to abolish the Irish Parliament, which ruled the country from Dublin. The British Prime Minister, William Pitt the Younger, was worried by the rebellion and the small French invasion which landed at Killala Bay in 1798, and wanted to strengthen British control over Ireland. In 1800 the Dublin Parliament voted itself out of existence by passing the Act of Union: Ireland became part of the United Kingdom. This was a decisive moment in Irish history. In the following century nationalists tried to undo the Act of Union, but many Irish Protestants became convinced that the union was in their interests.

The terms of the Act of Union

- Britain and Ireland to become a single kingdom joining Scotland, Wales, England and Ireland in the United Kingdom of Great Britain and Ireland.
- All laws for Ireland to be made in the Parliament at Westminster.
- The Irish Parliament to be abolished.
- Ireland to be represented in the United Kingdom Parliament by 100 MPs.
- Free trade to be established between Britain and Ireland.

Robert Emmet's rebellion, 1803

The union with Britain was opposed by many people in Ireland. A small group of Irishmen travelled to France to try to get support for a rebellion. They failed and on their return to Ireland they joined Robert Emmet in the unsuccessful rebellion of 1803. Emmet was executed but is remembered for his courtroom speech when he said, 'Let no man write my epitaph until my country takes her place among the nations of the earth.'

England
The cross of St George

Scotland
The cross of St Andrew

Ireland
The cross of St Patrick

United Kingdom

The new Union Jack flag of the United Kingdom, incorporating St Patrick's cross, first flown on 1 January 1801.

---

1 Look at Source C. What were Wolfe Tone's aims?

2 Make a list of the reasons for the failure of the 1798 rebellion.

Daniel O'Connell

In the years before the Act of Union, Protestants had been the pioneers of Irish nationalism. After 1800 a Catholic, Daniel O'Connell, became the leading Irish nationalist.

Who was O'Connell and what impact did he have on Irish nationalism?

Catholic Association

In 1793 Catholics who owned property had been given the right to vote but they were not allowed to become Members of Parliament. O'Connell organised the Catholic Association and encouraged huge numbers of poor Catholics to join by cutting the membership fee from 21 shillings a year to one shilling. The priests recommended that Catholics join O'Connell's Catholic Association. For the first time the Catholic Church became strongly associated with nationalism in Ireland.

Catholic Emancipation Act, 1829

O'Connell held meetings around the country. In 1828 he was elected to Parliament as MP for County Clare. This victory and the fear of a possible Catholic uprising forced the government to pass the Catholic Emancipation Act in 1829. Catholics could now become MPs. O'Connell had won a victory for Irish nationalism and he became known as the 'Liberator'.

Repeal of the Union

O'Connell was happy for Ireland to be ruled by the English monarch but he wanted to re-establish an Irish Parliament in Dublin. To achieve this he campaigned for the Act of Union to be removed. He and his followers held 'monster meetings' attended by hundreds of thousands of people, to put pressure on the British government. The largest meeting took place at Tara, County Meath, in 1843 when almost half a million people turned out to hear O'Connell speak.

Source A
Monster meeting at Clifden, County Galway, 20 September 1843.

Source B

O'Connell's speech at Tara, 1843. Tara was the old site of the High Kings of Ireland.

We are at Tara of the Kings. The strength and majority of the national movement was never shown so well as at this great meeting. The numbers are greater than any that ever gathered before in Ireland in peace or war. Such an army!

The failure of the repeal movement

The government banned the monster meetings and imprisoned O'Connell for a short while. In 1845 the movement for repeal of the Union was overshadowed by the failure of the potato crop and the resulting great famine in Ireland. O'Connell died in 1847.

Source C

Daniel O'Connell, 1775–1847

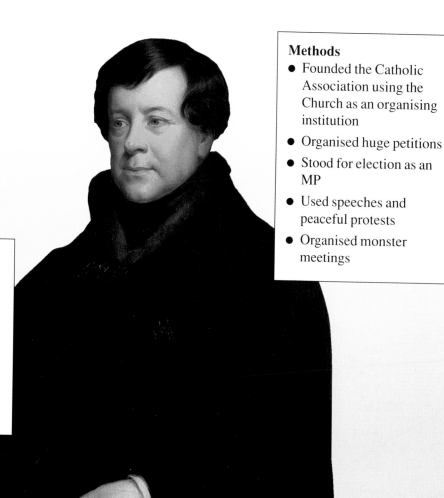

Methods
- Founded the Catholic Association using the Church as an organising institution
- Organised huge petitions
- Stood for election as an MP
- Used speeches and peaceful protests
- Organised monster meetings

Aims
- Catholic emancipation
- The right of more Catholics to vote
- The right of Catholics to sit in Parliament
- Repeal of the Union
- The right of Ireland to have its own Parliament

Results
- Became MP for County Clare in 1828
- Catholic Emancipation in England and Ireland in 1829
- Monster meetings banned, O'Connell imprisoned
- Repeal of the Union failed

Young Irelanders

Before his death O'Connell had been criticised by younger followers who wished to abandon peaceful protest and use force to end the Union. Thomas Davis, a graduate of Trinity College, Dublin, founded an organisation called Young Ireland which was non-sectarian (many of the leaders were Protestants) and believed that Ireland must be completely independent of England. The Young Irelanders were intellectuals who were strongly influenced by the ideas and example of the United Irishmen of 1798.

Young Ireland was inspired by revolutions in Italy, Germany and France in 1848 and John Mitchel, the son of a Presbyterian minister, argued in the newspaper, *The United Irishman*, for rebellion. This was not a good time to organise a revolution because Ireland was in the grip of famine but the Young Irelanders nevertheless planned a revolution. Led by William Smith O'Brien and lacking weapons and numbers, the rising was a disaster and finished in a skirmish in a cabbage garden in Tipperary. Mitchel and O'Brien were arrested and transported.

Source D

A modern historian's view of the Young Irelanders:

The Young Irelanders were full of revolutionary talk but they were isolated from the mass of the people; they had no aid from the Catholic Church's network, except from a few priests, and they did not wish to side outright with the peasants.

Liz Curtis, *The Cause of Ireland,* 1994

Source E

This 1848 engraving shows the Young Ireland rebels and local peasants besieging the house containing police in what has become known as the 'Battle of Widow McCormack's cabbage patch' at Ballingarry, County Tipperary

Interpretations of O'Connell

1 Look at Source A. Why might the government in London be concerned about these huge crowds? What action did they decide to take?

2 List three ways in which O'Connell differed from the United Irishmen.

3 Think about Daniel O'Connell's life and background. Why do you think he chose to fight for these two issues:
a Catholic emancipation – the right of Catholics to sit in Parliament?
b Repeal of the Union – the right of Ireland to govern herself?

4 What big difference might Catholic emancipation make in relation to who might have power in Ireland?

5 Why do you think fewer Protestants supported O'Connell than supported the United Irishmen?

6 How and why did nationalism become so strongly associated with Catholics during O'Connell's lifetime?

7 Why do you think Protestants became more in favour of the Union during O'Connell's lifetime?

3

The Great Famine

A great catastrophe overwhelmed Ireland in the 1840s. The potato crop, which was the only food of many people, became infected with a disease called potato blight. Many people starved to death or died from diseases caused by hunger.

Why did the Great Famine take place and how did it influence the development of Ireland?

The land

In 1800, families in the Irish countryside rarely owned the land that they farmed. Much of the land was owned by large landowners who did not live on their property. Instead, they rented the land out to tenants. Tenants, however, had no rights and landlords could increase rents or evict tenants from their land. Many families in the countryside lived in terrible conditions in damp and overcrowded cottages.

In Ireland, family land – even if it was rented – was traditionally divided up equally among the sons on the death of the father. This meant the size of farms became smaller with every passing generation. Those who did not have any land were known as landless labourers.

The population

A great rise in the Irish population in the late 18th and early 19th centuries increased the pressure on the land even more. As farms became even smaller there was an increase in the number of landless labourers. One reason for the population increase was that a family could live off a very small piece of land growing potatoes. People were getting married younger and having more children. By 1841, there were over 8 million people living in Ireland.

The potato

In the early 19th century, many Irish families depended almost entirely on the potato for food. Most of the other crops and livestock were sold to pay rent to the landlord. By 1845, about one-third of the population ate little except potatoes. They only occasionally ate meat, fish, or other vegetables.

Potatoes were easy to grow, even on poor soil, and they could produce a large yield on a small amount of land. They were also very nutritious.

Source B

The interior of a 19th-century cottage.

Source A – Census of Ireland, 1841

Farmers with over 15 acres	277,000
Farmers with under 15 acres	310,000
Cottiers with a smallholding	300,000
Labourers with no land	700,000

Causes of the Famine

Land

- most land was owned by English landlords
- most Irish were tenant farmers or landless labourers
- land was divided between families into smaller and smaller plots

Population growth

- younger marriages led to higher birth rate
- larger families led to more sub-division of land

Crops

- potatoes became the 'staple' diet
- small plots could produce large yields of potatoes
- when potatoes ran out, people went hungry until next harvest
- other crops sold to pay rent

Potato blight

- fungus attacked potatoes
- massive loss of crops 1845–1849
- few seed potatoes to plant for the next year

Source C

A government report on the conditions of landless labourers in 1845:

> In many districts their only food is the potato, their only drink water, their cabins are seldom a protection against the weather, a bed or a blanket is a rare luxury, and their pig and manure heap are their only property.

The Devon Commission Report, 1845

Source E
Children scrabbling for potatoes.

Source D
A mother and her children, starving during the Famine. The *Illustrated London News.*

Source F

The poverty of some crowded parts of the countryside was clear from a description of Gweedore, Donegal in 1837:

> None of their women can afford more than one shift [dress]. Nor can many of them afford a second bed. Whole families of grown-up sons and daughters of mature age sleep together with their parents, and all in the bare buff. Their beds are straw. If any gentleman should be sent here to investigate I can show him about 140 children bare naked during winter, and some hundreds covered only with filthy rags, most disgustful to look at.

Patrick McKye, *National School Teacher,* 1837

Source G

The discovery of the potato blight in Ireland, Daniel McDonald, 1821–1853

● *Give three reasons why there was a rise in the population of Ireland in the late 18th and early 19th centuries.*

Potato blight

In 1845, the potato crop was attacked by a mysterious fungus. The wind and the rain spread the fungus from place to place. It reduced the potatoes to a foul-smelling pulpy mess.

This was potato blight but neither scientists nor the people who grew potatoes knew what caused the blight or how to prevent it. When the potatoes were harvested in October, some areas in Ireland had no crop. It was estimated that almost half of the potato crop in Ireland had been ruined.

Source H

In 1846 a well-off Protestant described the potato blight:

I was startled to hear a rumour that all the potato fields in the district had been blighted and went out to visit my crop. I found them lush and in full blossom, promising a rich harvest. Five days later I returned to the potato fields. My feelings may be imagined when, before I saw the crop, I smelt the fearful stench. The stalks still looked green and healthy but I knew that the crop was worthless. Within hours the stalks had withered, the leaves decayed, the potatoes themselves rotten and the stench from so much rotten vegetation was almost unbearable.

Government reaction to the Famine

The blight re-appeared in the years after 1845. The food shortages caused by the blight resulted in a famine in Ireland. About one million people died of starvation or hunger-related diseases. Many of the people who died came from the poorest sections of society.

When the blight first appeared, Sir Robert Peel was the British Prime Minister. His government imported maize from America which was sold to the people who had lost their potato crop. The policy was successful. In 1845 and early 1846, nobody died of starvation.

In June 1846, Peel was replaced as Prime Minister by Lord John Russell. The government was worried that if they again bought food from America, it would ruin the trade of the Irish food merchants. At the end of 1846, the government decided to force people who needed money for food to do work like road-building. But people who were already weakened by hunger could not do physical work. The wages paid were also very low and not always enough to buy food. In the winter of 1846–1847, thousands of people died of hunger and disease in Ireland and many others emigrated.

Change of policy

In February 1847, the government changed its policies again and decided to distribute free food at soup-kitchens. In the summer of 1847, over three million people were given free food each day from the soup-kitchens. This new policy saved many lives.

In 1847, as the situation improved, the soup-kitchens were closed and the local workhouses had to provide relief. Starving people could live there and get food but they were dreadful places with strict rules, overcrowding and disease. The workhouses were paid for by local taxes instead of money from central government. Some landlords evicted their tenants to avoid paying more tax.

The blight continued in 1848 and 1849, although it was much worse in the west of the country where people continued to die. In these areas, evictions and emigration were also very high, even after the potato crop began to improve after 1851.

Consequences of the Famine

Population decrease
One million died of starvation and disease.

Language
Most of those who died spoke Irish. Irish became associated with poverty. Children were encouraged to learn English.

Emigration
One million emigrated to the USA, Australia and Britain. There was continuous emigration from Ireland for the next 100 years.

Bitterness
Many blamed Britain for what happened in Ireland. Anti-British resentment became strong, especially in the USA where many of the Irish emigrants settled. The Fenian Movement, a new form of revolutionary nationalism, was founded in the USA in 1858

The end of sub-division

The custom of sub-dividing was discouraged. Landlords preferred livestock farming to growing crops. They needed fewer workers. These developments further encouraged emigration.

Source I

Emigrant Ship by John Glenn Wilson. The ship is leaving Belfast for America.

1 Explain some of the causes of the Famine using the following headings:
● the way land was subdivided: tenants; rents; use of surplus food
● population growth
● landless labourers
● dependence on the potato; the blight.

2 List the various ways in which the government reacted to the Famine in Ireland. Explain some of the reasons why they changed their policies.

3 Describe some of the short-term and long-term effects of the Famine on Ireland.

4

The Fenians and the Home Rule Party – two types of nationalism

After the Great Famine, revolutionary nationalism and constitutional nationalism developed in Ireland. Both forms of nationalism continued to shape Irish politics into the 20th century.

What were the differences between these two types of Nationalism?

Revolutionary nationalism: the Fenian movement

After the failure of the Young Ireland rebellion in 1848, many of the leaders fled to France and America. One rebel, James Stephens, returned to Ireland from France in 1856. In 1858 he founded a new secret revolutionary group, the Irish Republican Brotherhood. At the same time, in America, a twin organisation was set up called the Fenian Brotherhood. The name came from the Irish word Fianna, who were a legendary band of Irish warriors. The IRB and Fenians aimed to use physical force to make Ireland an independent republic.

The Fenian rising, 1867

In 1867 the Fenians tried to organise a rebellion. Once again the result was a disaster, as the movement was betrayed by police informers. An attack on an arms depot in Chester in England failed and the leaders were arrested. In Ireland Fenians attacked the police in Dublin, Drogheda, Cork, Tipperary, Clare and Limerick but were easily defeated. Some were captured, others went on the run.

Source B

James Stephens (1824 – 1901) the founder of the Irish Republican Brotherhood.

Later in the same year some Fenians were arrested in Manchester. A week later they escaped from a police van which was ambushed by other Fenians. In the attack a policeman was shot dead. Three of the Fenians were arrested and hanged for murder. Their names were Allen, Larkin and O'Brien. None of them had fired the shot that killed the policeman and they became known as the Manchester Martyrs. The execution caused a wave of sympathy and nationalist feeling.

The Fenian rising was a failure but nationalists continued to seek independence through physical force or persuasion in Parliament.

Source A

The secret oath taken by IRB members:

I do solemnly swear in the presence of Almighty God that I will do my utmost, at every risk while life lasts, to make Ireland an independent, democratic republic. I will yield obedience in all things to the commands of my superior officers.

The Fenian attack on the prison van in Manchester. A modern artist's impression based on an *Illustrated London News* drawing of the time.

Constitutional nationalism: the struggle for Home Rule

Despite the failure of the Fenian rising in 1867, many people were persuaded that Ireland should have some form of independence. Isaac Butt, a Conservative Protestant, was the lawyer who had defended some of the Fenians in court. He was impressed by their political views but did not agree with the use of physical force. He founded the Irish Home Rule League in 1873 which later became the Irish Parliamentary Party, known as the Home Rule Party. The Irish Parliamentary Party tried to obtain an Irish Parliament in Dublin through peaceful and legal means. The Home Rulers were not seeking complete independence. They were loyal to the British government and the Union, but wanted Ireland to be given the right to make decisions about home affairs in a Dublin Parliament.

In 1874 the Home Rulers won 60 of the 103 Irish seats in Parliament. Many leading Fenians later became supporters of the Home Rule Party.

Source C

The views of a Fenian leader on Home Rule:

My principles have never altered, and I can see nothing wrong in my adapting to changed conditions. I was driven into Fenianism because it seemed likely to achieve success and what was called 'constitutional agitation' seemed hopeless. Now the position was reversed. Fenianism had collapsed and there seemed a prospect that a constitutional movement might succeed.

John Devoy, *Recollections of an Irish Rebel*, 1929

1 Look at Source A. What were the aims and methods of the Irish Republican Brotherhood?

2 What were the aims and methods of the Home Rulers?

3 Look at Source C. Explain how and why the writer's political views changed over time.

The origins of unionism

1 In the 19th century there was a great change in the political views of northern Protestants. The Belfast area became prosperous as new linen mills and shipyards were set up. Many Protestants came to think that their wealth depended on the link with Britain. They became known as unionists.

2 A powerful nationalist called Parnell dominated Irish politics in the 1880s. He called for limited independence or Home Rule for Ireland. He joined forces with Fenians and organised a campaign against landlords in the Irish countryside. This was called the Land War.

3 Gladstone, the leader of the Liberal Party, was persuaded that Home Rule for Ireland was a good idea. In 1886 Gladstone tried to pass a law bringing in Home Rule and setting up a Parliament in Dublin. The Liberal Party was divided by this and the law was not passed.

5 Ulster unionists were deeply shocked by the move towards Home Rule. They organised a vigorous campaign against Home Rule. They joined forces with the British Conservative Party.

4 Parnell's career was ruined by a scandal over his private life. He had an affair with a married woman. She was later divorced and Parnell married her. His party became divided by the affair and remained divided for many years.

Protestants and the Union

In the late 18th century some Ulster Presbyterians had been among the first Irish nationalists. While a small number of Protestants continued to support nationalism, during the 19th century most Protestants became supporters of the link with Britain. They became known as unionists because they wanted to maintain the parliamentary union with Britain.

Why did Protestants come to believe so strongly in the Union?

Religion

Most Ulster Protestants were the descendants of Protestant settlers from Scotland and England who had moved to Ireland in the 17th century. They sometimes described themselves as 'Ulster Scots'.

Most Ulster Protestants were either members of the Church of Ireland or Presbyterians. They saw the Catholic Church as an enemy of freedom because it gave so much power to its priests and bishops. They believed that the Catholic Church had too much influence on nationalists. They feared that a Dublin Parliament would be dominated by the views of the Catholic Church. These anti-Catholic ideas were strengthened by a new strict spirit that developed in the Protestant churches in the 19th century. In the 1820s and 1830s there was disagreement in the Presbyterian Church about how strict their faith should be. The argument was won by a preacher called Henry Cooke and his followers who wanted a stricter approach.

In 1798 some northern Presbyterians had taken part in the rebellion against the British. Under Cooke's leadership the Presbyterians rejected the ideas of the United Irishmen about equality between people of all faiths. They saw the link with Britain as a way of protecting their Protestant identity. Because nationalism under O'Connell came to be linked with the Catholic Church, many Protestants reacted against him.

HANDS OFF PRIEST!

Source B

This poster shows a priest with Erin tied in a noose.

● *Describe what is happening in the picture. How does the cartoon help us to understand Protestants' fears?*

Source A

When O'Connell, the Catholic nationalist, visited Belfast in 1841 he was strongly criticised by the Presbyterian leader, Henry Cooke.

> When you invade Ulster, and unfurl the flag of Repeal, you will find yourself in a new climate. I believe you are a great bad man, engaged in a great bad cause.

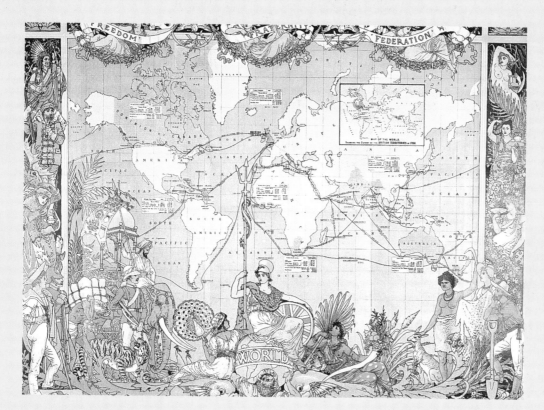

Source C

An illustrated 19th-century map showing the extent of the British Empire.

Unionism and economics

Unionists believed that they were much better off economically under the Parliament at Westminster. The wealthier farmers and landowners were mostly Protestant. They feared that a government in Dublin would give their land back to the Catholics whose ancestors owned it in the 17th century.

Change in the towns and cities

In the 18th and 19th centuries Britain experienced an Industrial Revolution. North-east Ulster, particularly Belfast and the Lagan Valley, was the only part of Ireland where there were major industrial developments. The rest of Ireland remained largely agricultural. The Ulster industrialists thought that most of the southern MPs would be from farming areas and would not understand or care about the needs of the industrial north. They also feared that a Dublin Parliament would endanger their markets in Britain and the Empire.

Working-class Protestants in the Belfast area also felt that they were better off being united with Britain. Jobs in the new mills, factories and shipyards offered better wages than they could get in the countryside. Most big businesses were owned by Protestants and they gave jobs to other Protestants. Working-class Protestants feared that they would lose this special position if they were ruled by a largely Catholic government in Dublin.

Pride in the Empire

Unionists believed that they had become prosperous not just because they were part of the United Kingdom, but because they were at the heart of a great trading empire. Both employers and workers felt that the strength of the Empire gave them peace and prosperity. They were afraid that if Ireland gained Home Rule then other parts of the Empire would want the same and the whole Empire would break up.

Using each of the following headings, give one reason why unionists opposed Home Rule:
- Religious fears
- Land fears
- Industrial benefits
- Benefits from the Empire

The Industrial Revolution in north-east Ulster

While the question of Home Rule was at the centre of the political debate, north-east Ulster was changing dramatically in economic terms. Belfast grew very rapidly from a small provincial port at the beginning of the 19th century into a large industrial and manufacturing city, the equal of Glasgow or Liverpool.

What changes took place in north-east Ulster during the 19th century?

Changes in the linen industry

Linen cloth had been produced in Ulster for centuries by people in their own homes, or in very small workplaces. At the end of the 18th century, new machines for spinning and weaving cotton were being used in England which produced cotton cloth more cheaply than hand-made linen. These machines were too large for cottages and were set up in factories.

Source A

Cottage Industry, 1791 by William Hincks (1752–97)

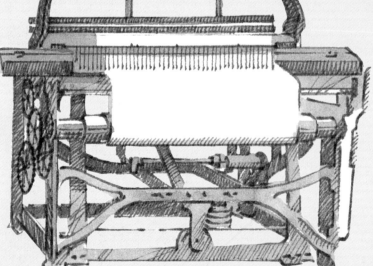

Source B

An illustration of a power loom – one of the large new machines which were set up in factories.

The linen mills

In the years after 1800 many people experimented with ways of machine-spinning the flax from which linen cloth was made. At first they were not successful but in 1825 an English inventor, James Kay, discovered that if flax was soaked long enough in water it was possible to pass the flax through machinery. When Mulholland's cotton mill in Belfast burned down in 1828, a huge mill for spinning linen yarn was built instead. In this five-storey building, steam engines powered over 15,000 spindles. It was a great success and was quickly copied elsewhere in Belfast and the Lagan Valley.

Numbers of people employed in the mills	
1840	8,000
1900	78,000

The linen yarn then had to be woven into cloth. Before 1850 most weaving took place on hand-looms in cottages. When power-looms for weaving linen were invented, many weaving factories were built. They were mainly situated near the Belfast docks where the factory owners could import the coal they needed for the steam-powered machines. There were also weaving factories outside Belfast, close to the railway lines and canals.

Source C
Women operating looms at York Street Mills, Belfast.

Developing Belfast's port

Belfast's Gaelic name, *Béal Féirste*, means 'the mouth of the sand banks'. It gives a good idea of why the harbour was not suitable for large ships. The River Lagan was very shallow and muddy right up to the Belfast quayside. This made it difficult and expensive to move heavy goods such as coal. Large ships had to anchor out in Belfast Lough in the deep water. All goods coming into the city and leaving it had to be loaded onto small 'lighter boats'.

The new Victoria Channel, which was opened in 1849, solved this problem. It was cut across the bends in the river to provide a straight passage and deep water. Large ships were now able to anchor right in the centre of the city.

New, larger quays, where large ships could dock, were built in the centre of Belfast. The steam engines which ran the mills needed to import 150,000 tonnes of coal every year from the coalfields of Britain. Cheap coal could now be taken by the network of canals and railways to all parts of the province. This provided cheap steam power for the machines and so the linen industry boomed in the second half of the century. Lisburn, Dungannon and Armagh all developed thriving linen mills and factories as a result.

Shipbuilding

The new access to deep water, and cheap and plentiful land nearby, made Belfast ideal for shipbuilding. In the 1850s, Edward Harland established a shipyard in a part of Belfast known as Queen's Island. He had a partner from Liverpool called Gustav Wolff and in 1861 the firm became known as Harland and Wolff. In that year the shipyard employed only 500 men but it went on to employ 14,000 by 1914, becoming the single biggest employer in Ulster.

The yard was at the forefront of technology, building at first iron and then steel ships. Many ships were built in the latter part of the century, most of them for the White Star Line in Liverpool. This was the era of luxury travel for people with money, and of emigration for the poor leaving Europe to make their fortunes in America. Belfast shipyard's greatest achievement in these years was the building in 1899 of Oceanic II, the largest ship in the world.

Source D

The *Olympic*, ready for launching, with the *Titanic* under construction on the left.

The growth of engineering

The development of the linen industry and shipbuilding led to the growth of another important manufacturing industry – engineering. Ships needed huge turbines and other kinds of engine to drive them. Thousands of wet-spinning frames and power-looms were required to produce the millions of yards of linen that were sold all round the world every year. Boilers to make the steam which powered these machines were also needed. Such machines were very expensive to import so an industry developed making them more cheaply at home. Harland and Wolff still brought in the sheets of steel from the Clyde in Scotland, but these were shaped in Belfast. Other foundry owners concentrated on producing textile machinery and boilers for the home market. Eventually, the Belfast engineering works became so successful that they were selling their products to other parts of the Empire. Machines for weaving jute and cotton were sent to India.

New industries

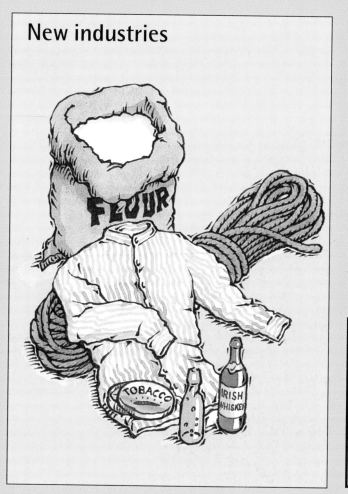

Effects of industrial growth

As Belfast grew rapidly, the working and living conditions that developed provided the background to an increase in sectarian feelings.

- Many people from the surrounding countryside came to Belfast looking for work either in the spinning mills or as weavers.
- They brought with them the sectarian rivalries and fears that had developed in the countryside.
- In 1800 Catholics were about 8 per cent of the population of Belfast. By 1840 they were about 32 per cent.
- Catholics and Protestants settled in separate areas of the city and did not mix socially.

By the end of the 19th century, Belfast had the largest shipyard, the largest ropeworks and the largest linen mill in the world. Yet there were continual sectarian outbreaks and rioting. Protestants generally worked in the better trades and more skilled jobs in the large companies. In 1864, nearly half of the 500 shipyard workers were Catholics but by 1887 the number of Catholic employees had decreased to 77, even though the total workforce had increased dramatically.

Riots, in which Catholics and Protestants fought, became a regular feature of life in Belfast. The first large-scale riots seem to have taken place in 1832 at election time. Protestant supporters of the winning candidates attempted to march through a largely Catholic area but were driven back by the Catholic residents. The police were called to quell the disturbance and opened fire. Two elderly men and two boys were killed. Other serious disturbances occurred in 1841, 1857, 1864, 1872 and 1886.

---

1 How did the Victoria Channel help the growth of Belfast?

2 Give three reasons for the growth of the linen industry in 19th century Ulster.

3 Why did shipbuilding and engineering become important industries in Belfast?

Life in Belfast

There was a great contrast in lifestyle in Victorian Belfast between the prosperous middle classes and ordinary workers.

Working hours were long, so workers needed to live as close as possible to their work. Their rows of houses, built in the shadow of the mills, were dark and dreary even in the summer. Wages were so poor that families had to share the cost of rents and this led to overcrowding and insanitary conditions, not helped by the poor standard of the houses. There were frequent outbreaks of cholera and typhus. Dr Spedding, medical officer in the Shankill area, reported that the houses of the factory workers were 'generally overcrowded, and badly ventilated, the chimney usually stuffed with straw. Very many families sleep three or four to a bed in a small, close apartment.' Another doctor reported: 'The diet of the factory hands consists of tea and white bread three times daily, sometimes I see butter used, sometimes not – potatoes or meat only rarely.'

Source E

This is the prosperous face of middle-class Belfast in the 19th century. For ordinary working people, life was very different.

Source F

Working class homes in Belfast. Note how close the people live to the factories and the bare feet of the children.

Working conditions

Conditions in the mills were very hard. It was not until after 1874 that women and children had their hours cut to ten on each weekday and six on Saturday. Most factory workers were poorly paid. Mill and factory workers were paid less than textile workers in the rest of Britain. Women were paid considerably less than men. Wages could be reduced by the payment of fines for a number of offences.

There were also very serious health hazards. The damp, humid atmosphere which was required to keep the linen yarn from breaking affected the lungs of the spinning-room girls, especially when they came from the heat of the mill to the cold in the streets. The army would not accept men who had worked combing the raw flax because they often had serious lung disease.

Source G

The Belfast City Surgeon described the normal appearance of mill workers in 1877:

When they are about 30 years of age their appearance begins to alter, the face gets an anxious look, shoulders begin to get rounded – in fact they become prematurely aged and the greatest number die before 45 years.

1 How and why did the population of Belfast change during the 19th century?

2 What factors led to rioting in Belfast in the 19th century?.

3 You are a Health Inspector in 19th-century Belfast. Write a report giving details of the living conditions and working conditions of poor mill workers.

7

Parnell and Home Rule

From the 1870s to the 1890s, Irish politics was dominated by Charles Stewart Parnell and the struggle for Home Rule.

How did Parnell contribute to Irish nationalism?

After Isaac Butt's death in 1879, the new leader of the Irish Parliamentary Party was Charles Stewart Parnell, a Protestant landowner from County Wicklow who had been educated in England. He was concerned that the British government could easily ignore the Irish Party at Westminster. He organised the Irish MPs into making long speeches to hold up the business of Parliament. A new crisis in the Irish countryside provided Parnell with the opportunity to get support for the Home Rule Party.

In the 1870s the price of food dropped and many Irish tenant farmers were unable to sell their crops and pay their rent. Large numbers of smallholders in the west of Ireland were evicted. Between 1877 and 1879 the potato blight returned and famine once more threatened the country. The farming crisis led to a renewed struggle between the landlords and the tenants.

Source A

Charles Stewart Parnell 1846–1891. An illustration from *Vanity Fair*.

Source B

Eviction in the west of Ireland, 1881. Compare this photograph to the painting by Lady Butler on the cover of this book.

● *Which picture do you think is more realistic? What impression is the artist trying to portray in each picture? Which picture is more useful as evidence of eviction in the 19th century?*

The Land League

Parnell decided to make use of the anger among poor farmers to support his calls for Home Rule. He was not the only politician to see the farming crisis as a chance for political action. The Fenians also decided to gather recruits for their cause. An old Fenian, Michael Davitt, returned home to Mayo in the west of Ireland in 1878. He helped to organise the tenants to try to get fair rents and an end to the evictions. Parnell negotiated with Davitt in 1879 and they agreed to act together. A new organisation was set up called the Land League. Both Parnell and Davitt played leading parts in the running of the League. Thousands of poor smallholders in the west of Ireland joined the League. Supporters of the League took direct action to break the power of the landlords. Sometimes this led to violence. This campaign became known as the Land War.

The Land War

The Land League organised mass demonstrations. Some branches tried to negotiate with the landlords for a lower rent when the harvests were poor. They published the names of sympathetic landlords in the local paper. At some of the meetings they burnt the leases (records of the rent agreement) given by harsh landlords. Sometimes members of the League took the law into their own hands and threatened landlords. One landlord, Lord Mountmorris, was waylaid and killed in County Galway in 1880.

Many landlords did not live in the area or were well protected and could not be attacked. So the League members turned on local people who co-operated with the landlords. After an eviction a new family was often prepared to pay the landlord's price. They moved onto a farm as soon as the previous tenants had been evicted. League members were unpleasant to these families and to those tenants who paid the full rent.

Source C

A Land League banner showing Charles Stewart Parnell. The other side has a picture of Michael Davitt.

Source D

A dramatic illustration of the time showing the murder of Lord Mountmorris by Land League assassins

35

Boycotting

Parnell's advice was to isolate bad landlords and new tenants who took over the farms of evicted families. The manager of the estate on which this tactic was first tried was called Captain Boycott, and so the tactic of putting pressure on someone by ignoring them became known as 'boycotting'.

Source E

Parnell explained his policy of isolating or 'boycotting' in a speech made in 1880

You must show him when you meet him, in the street of the town, at the shop counter, in the fair or market place, and even in the house of worship, by leaving him severely alone, by putting him into a moral Coventry, by isolating him as if he was a leper of old, you must show him your detestation of the crime he has committed.

Gladstone's Land Act

In 1881 Gladstone, the British Prime Minister, brought in a new law known as the Land Act which guaranteed a fair rent for tenants. Gladstone admitted that he only brought in this law because of pressure from the Land League. Although he was against violence, Parnell was friendly with many Fenians. By 1881 the Land War was becoming more violent. The government blamed Parnell and he was imprisoned in Kilmainham Gaol, Dublin for several months. During this time the level of violence in the countryside further increased. Parnell was finally released in return for a promise to support Gladstone's land reforms and to try to stop the violence in the countryside.

A few days after his release two civil servants, Lord Frederick Cavendish and his assistant, Thomas Burke, were stabbed to death in Phoenix Park, Dublin by a Fenian group that called itself the Irish National Invincibles. The government suspected that Parnell was involved. In fact, Parnell had nothing to do with these murders.

The First Home Rule Bill – 1886

In 1885, Parnell's Home Rule Party gained 86 of the 103 Irish seats in Parliament and could now influence the two big parties – the Conservatives and the Liberals. Parnell helped to convince Gladstone that a Home Rule Parliament would solve the Irish problem. The First Home Rule Bill was introduced by Gladstone in 1886. It aimed to give limited power to a Dublin Parliament. The Bill was defeated when 93 Liberals voted with the Conservatives against it. The Conservatives then took power.

Source F

Gladstone and the Land League 1881.

● *Why, according to the cartoonist is Gladstone producing a land bill for Ireland?*

The Divorce scandal

For some years Parnell had been involved with a married woman, Kitty O'Shea. When their relationship was made public, this caused a split in the Parliamentary Party. At that time divorce was rare and was frowned upon by most people. Gladstone himself said that he could no longer deal with Parnell and that the Irish Party would have to choose another leader. Parnell refused to resign, which caused a split in nationalist opinion. The Catholic Church was very critical and Parnell was condemned in public by many priests. Parnell married Kitty O'Shea and continued to travel around Ireland to put his case but he became very ill and died on 6 October 1891, aged 45.

Source G
Kitty O'Shea.

Source H

This source is taken from a sermon delivered by a priest in a church near Avondale, Parnell's home.

Parnellism is a simple love of adultery and all those who profess Parnellism profess to love and admire adultery. Therefore I say to you, as parish priest, beware of these Parnellites for their cause is not patriotism, it is adultery.

Parnell and the Ulster Protestants

Parnell had underestimated the opposition of Protestants in Ulster to Home Rule. He saw the Protestants as a minor obstacle to political change. He thought that after initial protests they would accept a Dublin government.

Source I

Gladstone and his Liberals made the same mistake:

In Ulster the great majority of the people who are opposed to Home Rule will, when Home Rule is granted, forget past differences.

Liberal Party Report, 1887

Source J

Parnell and the unionists – a historian's view

Ulster unionists were unconvinced by Parnell's promise that the 'Irish people' accepted Home Rule as a final settlement. Parnell's description of the unionists as a 'miserable gang who trade upon the name of religion' was arrogant and insulting.

R. Foster, *Modern Ireland,* 1988

---

1 a What methods were used by the Land League during the Land War?
b Design a Land League poster urging tenants to boycott landlords.

2 What were the main points of Gladstone's Land Act of 1881?

3 Describe the methods used by Parnell to obtain Home Rule.

4 Explain Parnell's attitude towards Ulster unionists.

5 What were the effects of Parnell's divorce scandal?

8

Unionists and the Home Rule crisis

Both Parnell and Gladstone underestimated the Protestants of Ulster. When Gladstone promised Home Rule for Ireland in 1886, many Irish Protestants decided to organise an energetic campaign against it. Ulster was the centre of resistance.

How did northern unionists react to the First Home Rule Bill?

A number of societies were formed to show unionist hostility to Home Rule. In 1886 the Ulster Loyalist Anti-Repeal Union was formed to co-ordinate all the different unionist groups. It used the Orange Order, which had branches across the country, to help to get organised, and made all Protestant clergymen in Ulster honorary members.

Source A

The Orange Order played an important part in the protests against Home Rule. On 26 April 1886 a meeting of 20,000 Orangemen declared:

> We shall not acknowledge that Home Rule government; we shall refuse to pay taxes imposed by it; and we will resist to the uttermost all attempts to enforce such payments.

Source B

A modern historian describes the growing influence of the Orange Order at this time:

> Immediately the Orange Order became highly respectable and exceedingly powerful, for people of every class swelled its ranks – country gentlemen, Protestant clergymen, businessmen, tradesmen, labourers, farmers.

David Hammond, *Two Centuries of Irish History*, 1966

Unionists and Conservatives

Leaders of the British Conservative Party joined forces with the Ulster Protestants to try to defeat Gladstone. This was the beginning of an important alliance between the Conservatives and the unionists that was to last for over a hundred years. One Conservative, Lord Randolph Churchill, went to Belfast in February 1886 to show his support for the local unionists. He was greeted by enthusiastic crowds as he got off the boat at Larne and he announced to the great crowds turned out in Belfast to hear him speak that 'Ulster will fight, and Ulster will be right.' In his speech he made it clear that he saw Home Rule as a threat to the Empire and to the security of Britain.

Source C

On you it primarily rests whether Ireland shall remain an integral portion of this great empire sharing in its glory, partaking of all its strength, benefiting by all its wealth or whether, on the other hand, Ireland shall become the focus and the centre of foreign influence and deadly conspiracy.

Randolph Churchill, 22 February 1886

● *Why did Randolph Churchill feel that unionists were important to the British Empire?*

As a result of the Home Rule crisis the MPs elected by northern unionists began to organise themselves better. Led by Edward Saunderson these MPs formed themselves into a distinct parliamentary group in January 1886. This was the birth of the Ulster Unionist Party.

Anti-Home Rule Riots, 1886

Working-class unionists in Belfast took more direct action to show their opposition to Home Rule. Before Parliament voted on the Home Rule Bill in June 1886, rioting broke out between Catholics and Protestants in Belfast. Catholic workmen building a dock attacked a Protestant. In response an army of Protestant shipyard workers came down to the dock. A government report later described how the Catholics tried to get away.

Source D

The majority sought refuge in the River Lagan which runs by the dock. About twenty got on a raft. Others tried to escape by swimming. Some were soon in danger of drowning. One man returned to the shore and was badly beaten by the Island men, who also continued throwing stones at the men in the water. One lad named Curran was drowned.

The riots continued even after Parliament rejected the Home Rule Bill. When news reached Belfast of the defeat of the Bill, Protestant workers left work early to start celebrating. Orange Order bands played and marched and bonfires were lit. Some Catholic pubs were burnt out. Extra police were brought in from the south to reinforce the local constables. Many of these police were Catholics. The Protestant rioters attacked these policemen with paving stones. The police responded with baton charges and gunfire. The riots went on for weeks and by mid-September more than thirty people had been killed.

Source E
An illustration of a riot in 1886.

● *You are a journalist in Belfast in 1886. Write a report of the riot.*

---

1 What methods did unionists and the Orange Order use to organise resistance to the First Home Rule Bill in 1886?

2 Draw a timeline showing the key events and unionist organisations between 1886 and 1893.

1890–1914

1 There were few political changes in Ireland between 1890 and 1905. The Conservatives were in power most of the time. They supported the Union. They introduced important land reforms. The Liberals were briefly in power in the early 1890s; in 1893 they introduced another Home Rule Bill but it was blocked by the House of Lords.

2 The Gaelic League and the Gaelic Athletic Association were formed. They encouraged pride in the Irish language and Gaelic culture. Most ordinary members were Catholics. During these years there was a great upsurge of interest in poetry and art in Ireland among educated people. Many of the leading writers and artists were southern Protestants.

3 Most nationalists supported the Irish Parliamentary Party on Home Rule. A journalist called Arthur Griffith set up a small new party called Sinn Féin in 1905. Sinn Féin wanted Ireland to be less dependent on Britain. It had very few supporters. In Dublin and Belfast some working people became socialists. The socialists were led by Jim Larkin and James Connolly.

4 Between 1910 and 1914 there was a renewed argument about Home Rule. A Liberal government reduced the power of the House of Lords. The Lords were no longer able to block Home Rule indefinitely. A Home Rule Bill was passed by the House of Commons in 1912. The Lords could only delay a Dublin Parliament for two years. People signed the covenant in Ulster on 28 September 1912 to protest against Home Rule.

5 Ulster unionists got ready to fight against Home Rule. They set up a private army called the Ulster Volunteer Force. They were led by Edward Carson and James Craig.

6 By 1914 Ireland was close to civil war. The nationalists copied the unionists and set up an army to fight for Home Rule, called the Irish Volunteers. The outbreak of the First World War ended the crisis. Many men on both sides joined the British army to fight against Germany.

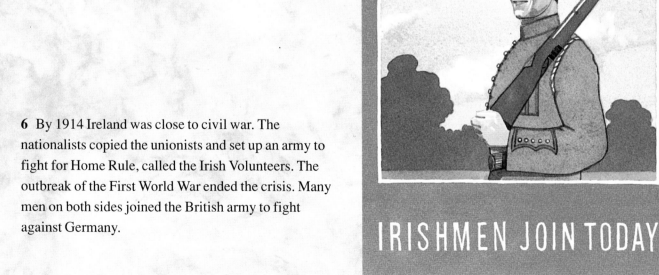

IRISHMEN JOIN TODAY

9

Tranquil years?

From 1886 to 1906, after the Home Rule crisis of 1886 and the fall of Parnell, Irish politics entered a quieter phase. Issues such as the question of land, which had caused so many problems, seemed to have been solved. Many people, Catholic and Protestant, turned their attention to a revival of Gaelic culture.

How did the cultural revival contribute to the development of Irish nationalism?

After the excitement of the 1880s, Irish politics entered a less dramatic phase at the end of the 19th and the start of the 20th centuries. Between 1886 and 1906 the Conservatives were in power most of the time. In 1893 a Unionist Clubs' Council was formed to organise unionists at grass-roots level and very soon about two hundred of these had been formed across the country. These clubs promoted unionism in Ireland but also tried to promote the cause in Great Britain. In the same year the Ulster Defence Union was formed. This represented a wide range of Ulster unionism and would provide leadership in future resistance to Home Rule. There was talk among its members of drilling and arming themselves.

The Second Home Rule Bill

This period of Conservative power was interrupted in 1892 when Gladstone and the Liberals came back to power. The following year Gladstone tried to bring in Home Rule for the second time and once again the unionists of Ulster organised an energetic campaign against it. The Home Rule Bill was passed by the House of Commons in 1893. However, the House of Lords, which was dominated by Conservatives, had the power to stop Home Rule. A year later Gladstone retired, having failed in his mission to set up a Home Rule Parliament for Ireland.

Conservative policy in Ireland

The aim of Conservative policy in Ireland was described at the time as 'killing Home Rule with kindness'. This meant making Ireland a peaceful and prosperous place so that support for nationalism would fade away. The greatest achievement of these years was the Land Act of 1903. This encouraged landlords to sell their estates. The government agreed to arrange the purchase of the land which they sold to the tenant farmers. Tenant farmers were able to borrow money for the purchase at a low rate of interest, repayable over many years. Many landlords disappeared and the land issue, which had dominated Irish politics for so long, became less of a problem.

The Conservatives also tried to introduce some small industries in poor areas. Their schemes included building harbours, encouraging fishing and fish-curing and expanding small cottage industries.

While the Conservatives tackled the question of the land, they did nothing to change the discrimination that Catholics faced in looking for work in the towns. The scale of discrimination was revealed by the 1901 census. In Belfast at that time, Catholics made up a quarter of the population but they had only about 10 per cent of the better-paid jobs such as shipyard work, boilermaking and engine making. Catholics tended to be found in poorly paid jobs such as dock work and female work in the linen mills.

Source A
'We will not have Home Rule',
Ulster convention, 1892.

The Gaelic revival – new forms of nationalism

In the years after the failure of the Home Rule Bill, some people became deeply interested in Gaelic culture. By encouraging the use of the Irish language (Gaelic) and traditional Irish games, songs and literature, they hoped that people in Ireland would see themselves as having their own Irish identity. This is a form of nationalism called 'cultural nationalism'.

In 1884 the Gaelic Athletic Association (GAA) was formed to encourage young people to play traditional Irish games such as hurling, Gaelic football and handball. Their rules banned members from playing British games like soccer, rugby and cricket. A national stadium was built in Dublin, called after the Catholic Archbishop Croke. Young people who began by playing in a local league could hope to win an all-Ireland medal at Croke Park.

The Gaelic League

In 1893 Eoin MacNeill, an Antrim Catholic, and Douglas Hyde, the son of a Protestant rector from Roscommon, set up the Gaelic League to encourage more people to learn and speak the Irish language. Hyde wrote down many Gaelic poems and songs and translated them into English. Hyde and MacNeill wanted the organisation to be non-political and open to both Protestants and Catholics.

The Gaelic League was also involved in a revival of traditional dance. Members of the League found out about the old country dances but changed them to their idea of what Irish dance should be. They made the dances more formal and less lively than when they were danced in the countryside.

Source C
Irish dancers.

Source B
Hurley players.

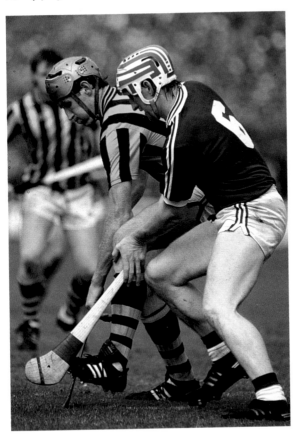

The literary revival

There was a great upsurge of interest in poetry and art among educated people, especially if it was connected with Irish culture. Many southern Protestants were very involved in the literary revival. Lady Gregory opened her home at Coole Park in Sligo to promising young writers like William Butler Yeats, the poet and dramatist, who wrote some of his most beautiful poetry there.

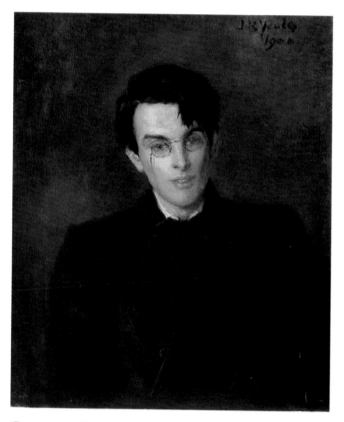

Source D
W. B. Yeats, 1865–1939.

The Abbey Theatre

Lady Gregory also founded the Abbey Theatre in Dublin so that Irish people could go and watch plays by Irish writers performed by Irish actors and actresses. Yeats wrote some plays based on Irish myths and legends which were performed at the Abbey. Some of the plays at the Abbey Theatre were criticised by Catholic nationalists because they did not fit in with the Catholic Church's teaching. There was a heated argument in 1907 when the play *The Playboy of the Western World* by J. M. Synge was first performed. The play showed a very earthy view of Irish country life and some Catholics felt that it was obscene and an insult to Irish people.

Source E
J. M. Synge, 1871–1909.

1 What was meant by the phrase 'killing Home Rule with kindness'? How did the Conservatives try to do this?

2 a What were the two main organisations involved in the Gaelic Revival?
b What did they try to achieve?

3 How did the Gaelic Revival contribute to Irish nationalism?

10

New political ideas

While nationalism and unionism continued to dominate Irish politics, new political movements began to emerge towards the end of the 19th century.

How popular were these new movements in Ireland?

While life improved for some people who lived in the countryside, life in the cities remained hard for ordinary people. Dublin, the Irish capital, had some of the worst slums in Europe. Of a total population of 350,000, one-third lived in one-room tenements. Those with jobs worked very long hours for low wages. Sickness and disease from insanitary conditions and poor food added to their hardships. In the first years of the 20th century Dublin had the worst death rate of any city in Europe.

Source A
James Larkin (1876–1947)

Source B
James Connolly (1868–1916)

Socialism

Many working people in many of the cities of western Europe turned to a new political movement called socialism which offered hope of an improvement. Socialists believed that the wealth of a country should belong to all the people. They believed that working-class people needed to join together in trade unions to fight for fair wages and working conditions, whatever their religion.

James Larkin and James Connolly tried to bring these ideas to the working people of Ireland. Larkin and Connolly had some success in persuading people of both faiths to join unions. However, they made very little progress in getting working men to vote for socialists rather than nationalist or unionist parties. While in Britain a new Labour Party developed to speak for the working classes, in Ireland socialists made little impact.

Sinn Féin

In the years between 1890 and 1914, nationalist politics was dominated by the Irish Parliamentary Party, with its commitment to some kind of Home Rule. Few people were attracted to the more radical idea of republicanism. A journalist called Arthur Griffith tried to change this. He founded a new party, called Sinn Féin, in 1905. The party's name means 'we ourselves' in Gaelic. Griffith wanted to see an Ireland that was completely free from the power of the Parliament at Westminster, but he was against violence. He believed that Irish MPs should just ignore Westminster and form their own Parliament in Dublin. But he believed that Ireland should remain within the British Empire with the King as head of state. Sinn Féin contested a by-election in North Leitrim in 1908 and lost. It was a very small organisation and had hardly any support outside Dublin before 1914.

Source C
Arthur Griffith (1871–1922)

Source D

The Irish Suffragette, Meg Connery, attempting to hand a leaflet to Bonar Law as he leaves a meeting with Edward Carson.

The women's movement

During the 19th century the increased right to vote had been limited to men only. At the start of the 20th century many women were beginning to seek the right to vote and become involved in socialist movements and trade unions. Inspired by the women's suffrage movement in England, two Irish women, Hanna Sheehy Skeffington and Margaret Cousins, set up the Irish Women's Franchise League 1908 which campaigned to give women the right to vote. Irish women, along with other women in the United Kingdom, had to wait until 1918 for the right to vote in elections.

---

1 Describe the living conditions of the poor in Dublin at the beginning of the 20th century.

2 Design a poster to show socialist aims.

3 What were the aims of: (a) Sinn Féin and (b) the women's movement

---

11

The Third Home Rule Bill

As long as a Conservative government remained in power there would be no Home Rule for Ireland. After many years of Conservative power, the Liberals won a great victory in the 1906 General Election but it was not until 1912 that a third Home Rule Bill was introduced.

Why was the third Home Rule Bill introduced in 1912?

The Conservatives lose power

When the Liberals returned to power in 1906, the Irish Parliamentary Party, with a new generation of Irish MPs, was reunited under the leadership of John Redmond. As long as the Conservatives were in power there could be no Home Rule. Now it became possible under the Liberals.

At first Redmond and the Irish Parliamentary Party were disappointed by the new Liberal government. The new Liberal Prime Minister, Henry Campbell-Bannerman, was not very keen on Home Rule and many Liberal politicians did not think it was very important. But although Home Rule was not a priority for the new government, unionists were still worried that their friends, the Conservatives, were out of power.

Source A

John Redmond: 1856–1918, an illustration from *Vanity Fair*

Lords versus Commons

The new Liberal government wanted to bring in a number of social reforms. In 1906 they had a very large majority in the House of Commons but their proposals were repeatedly rejected by the House of Lords. The Conservatives dominated the House of Lords and they used their power to block the new laws. The strain between the two Houses came to a head in 1909 when David Lloyd George, the Chancellor of the Exchequer, introduced a budget which included new taxes on land. It was impossible to get the Bill passed in the House of Lords because these men were the wealthiest landowners in the country and they would not pass a Bill that would increase their taxes.

The Liberals, led by the Prime Minister, Herbert Asquith, were furious that unelected lords were able to stop the work of an elected government. The Liberal government called two General Elections in 1910, to try to get support from the people in their bid to control the House of Lords. In fact they lost their huge majority in the House of Commons and were not strong enough to govern on their own. In future they had to depend on the support of the Irish Parliamentary Party and the Labour Party.

Election results in 1906 and 1910

	Liberals	Conservatives/ Unionists	Labour	Irish Nationalists
1906	400	157	30	83
1910*	272	272	42	84

* results for the second election in 1910

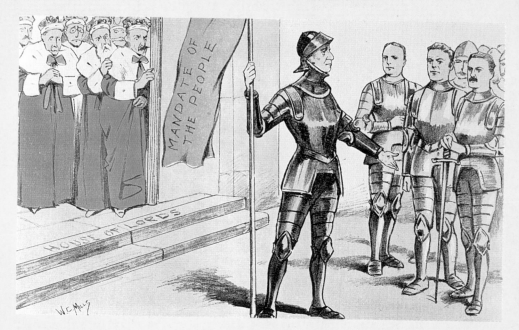

Source B

This cartoon was drawn in 1910. The man in the middle is Asquith, the Prime Minister.

● *How has the artist presented the conflict between the House of Lords and the House of Commons?*

● *Which side do you think the artist supports? Give reasons for your answer.*

Parliament Act 1911

The Liberals immediately introduced a Parliament Act to cut the power of the House of Lords. The new king threatened that if they did not agree, he would create more Liberal lords. The new law stated that the House of Lords could no longer stop the Commons from bringing in laws, it could only delay new laws for two years.

The rebirth of Home Rule

The election of 1910 was good news for Redmond and the Irish Party. The fall in support for the Liberal Party in England meant that it could not outvote all the other parties in the House of Commons. It needed support from a smaller party – and the Irish Parliamentary Party was happy to help – in return for a deal on Home Rule. For years it had seemed that the House of Lords was a permanent barrier in the way of Home Rule. After the Parliament Act of 1911 the House of Lords could only delay but not permanently reject an Irish Home Rule Bill.

The Third Home Rule Bill, 1912

The Liberals kept their word. In 1912 the government introduced a Home Rule Bill in the Commons as they had promised, and the reduced power of the House of Lords meant it would become law in 1914. Nationalists

were delighted. At last it seemed that the Dublin Parliament would be restored.

● There would be two houses in the Parliament in Dublin: a Senate, which would have similar powers to the House of Lords, and a more powerful chamber called the House of Commons.

● This Parliament would make laws on issues like education, agriculture and transport.

● The Parliament at Westminster would remain in charge of defence, foreign affairs and aspects of taxation.

---

1 Why were the Liberals angry with the House of Lords in 1909?

2 Look at the election results in 1910.
a Why did the Liberals need the support of the Irish Party to pass laws?
b What did the Liberals promise the Irish Party in return for their votes, and how did they keep their promise?

3 In what way did the Parliament Act change the power of the Lords?

4 Construct a diagram to show the terms of the third Home Rule Bill, 1912.

12

Towards civil war

Nationalists who thought that the 1912 Home Rule Bill would become law without much fuss two years later, were mistaken. Unionists carried out a powerful campaign between 1912 and 1914 to try to prevent the Bill becoming law, and to stop the establishment of a Home Rule Parliament in Dublin.

How did Ireland come close to civil war between 1912 and 1914?

Source A
Sir Edward Carson (1854–1935)

The unionists were led by two very able men. The most famous of these was Sir Edward Carson, a Protestant from Dublin and a brilliant lawyer with a successful career as a barrister in London. He was an excellent speaker who brought his courtroom style to his speeches both in Parliament and at public meetings. He wanted the whole of Ireland to stay part of the United Kingdom and he thought that the resistance of Ulster unionists would be enough to get the government to abandon all thoughts of Home Rule.

The other leading unionist was James Craig. He was a northern businessman, born just outside Belfast to a wealthy family of distillers. He became a stockbroker and MP in his native city. Craig's talents lay in organisation, very often behind the scenes. Carson himself said: 'James Craig did all the work and I got all the credit.' Although very different in upbringing and temperament, the two men worked well together. Carson led the resistance in Westminster in a number of the fiery speeches for which he was famous.

Source C
Sir James Craig (1871–1940)

Source B

The Tories had been enemies of Home Rule since 1886. In 1912 their leader, Bonar Law, saw the fight for the Union as part of his mission in political life.

I can imagine no lengths of resistance to which Ulster can go which I should not be prepared to support.

I said earlier it is impossible to grant Home Rule. The opposition of Ulster makes it impossible. I was present last week at a gathering in Belfast. It was the expression of the soul of a people. They say they will not submit except by force.

The support of the Protestant masses

The organisation of unionists was helped by the setting up of an Ulster Unionist Council in 1905. It brought together local unionist associations, the Orange Order and MPs. In the years 1910–1914 it was responsible for organising resistance from Ulster. The Council organised protest meetings through which ordinary people were able to show their opposition to Home Rule. The largest of the meetings were held at the showgrounds at Balmoral, in Belfast. Tens of thousands of people attended these gatherings. At all of them the message was the same: the Protestants of Ulster would use any means to stop rule from Dublin.

Source D

This propaganda postcard shows the leaders of the anti-Home Rule campaign.

- *Why do you think it also shows a picture of King William III?*

The Solemn League and Covenant

As a way of showing how strongly they felt, on 28 September 1912 almost a quarter of a million men left their places of work and marched to a number of centres to sign a 'Solemn League and Covenant' which explained why they were determined to resist Home Rule. Unionist women signed their own version separately. This became known as Ulster Day. It hinted that military force might be necessary to prevent a Home Rule Parliament in Ireland.

Source E

The Solemn League and Covenant said that:

- Home Rule would be disastrous for the prosperity of Ulster

- it would threaten civil and religious freedom

- it would threaten the Empire.

Therefore the people who opposed it would:

- stand together to defend their place in the United Kingdom

- use all means necessary to stop a Parliament being set up in Dublin

- refuse to accept the authority of such a Parliament.

Ulster's Solemn League and Covenant.

Being convinced in our consciences that Home Rule would be disastrous to the material well-being of Ulster as well as of the whole of Ireland, subversive of our civil and religious freedom, destructive of our citizenship and perilous to the unity of the Empire, we, whose names are underwritten, men of Ulster, loyal subjects of His Gracious Majesty King George V., humbly relying on the God whom our fathers in days of stress and trial confidently trusted, do hereby pledge ourselves in solemn Covenant throughout this our time of threatened calamity to stand by one another in defending for ourselves and our children our cherished position of equal citizenship in the United Kingdom and in using all means which may be found necessary to defeat the present conspiracy to set up a Home Rule Parliament in Ireland. And in the event of such a Parliament being forced upon us we further solemnly and mutually pledge ourselves to refuse to recognise its authority. In sure confidence that God will defend the right we hereto subscribe our names. And further, we individually declare that we have not already signed this Covenant.

The above was signed by me at _____
"Ulster Day." Saturday, 28th September, 1912.

_____

_____

God Save the King.

The Ulster Volunteer Force

When the unionists realised that Asquith and the Liberal government were keeping to the plan to have Home Rule for the whole of Ireland, Carson and other leading unionists decided to put more pressure on Westminster by establishing a unionist army. The Orange Order already had a well-structured organisation and in 1913 unionist leaders formed the Ulster Volunteer Force (UVF) to fight against Home Rule. With around 100,000 men joining the new force, the UVF outnumbered the British army in Ireland if it came to confrontation. Local landowners and businessmen very often took responsibility for the training of recruits using imitation wooden rifles because real weapons were scarce.

During the Home Rule crises of 1886 and 1893, the unionist leaders had used peaceful, constitutional methods. They now decided that they needed to prepare to fight and plans were made to smuggle in large quantities of arms from Germany to be distributed across the province.

Source G

Edward Carson inspecting the Ulster Volunteer Force, 1914.

The Larne gunrunning

The Ulster Unionist Council authorised Major Frederick Crawford to buy guns in Germany and these were then put ashore at various small northern ports. The most successful landing was at Larne on 24 April 1914, when the *Clyde Valley* unloaded arms without any sign of the authorities. The weapons were very quickly put into motorcars and spirited away to safe houses across the province. It was very well organised and the UVF gained about 24,000 rifles and 3 million rounds of ammunition.

Source F

As late as 1913 the nationalist leader, Redmond, said:

> Nobody denies that a riot may be attempted in Belfast and one or two other towns, but nobody in Ulster, outside a certain number of fanatics and leaders, believes in any organised rebellion.

Source H

The guns being unloaded at Larne.

Plans for self-government

The unionists also had a plan to govern themselves if Home Rule was established, and they had even appointed a group of men who would be responsible for governing the province in the event of Home Rule being imposed.

Source I

We must be prepared the morning Home Rule passes, to become responsible for the government of the Protestant Province of Ulster.

Carson at a demonstration at James Craig's house 'Craigavon', 1911

Source J

I said to him [Churchill] that most certainly the moment that the Home Rule Bill was passed you would not only set up your own government, but that you would allow no force of any kind in your area except the force appointed by you.

Letter from Bonar Law to Carson, September 1913

The nationalist response – the Irish Volunteers

Although they completely disagreed with them politically, nationalists were impressed by the way the unionists had armed themselves. Some leading nationalists decided that if the unionists were armed they must also get weapons. Nationalists established their own military organisation, the Irish Volunteer Force, in November 1913. While the Ulster Volunteer Force was pledged to fight against a Dublin government, the Irish Volunteers were formed to fight for Home Rule. It attracted members of the GAA and the Gaelic League and soon had about 80,000 members.

The Howth gunrunning

The Irish Volunteers also organised some gunrunning, though this was not as successful as in the North. Some wealthy supporters offered their private yachts to bring in guns. One of these was the writer, Erskine Childers. He was an excellent sailor and used his yacht, the *Asgard*, to smuggle in guns from Germany to the port of Howth, near Dublin. They were landed on 26 July 1914. The authorities were aware of the landing and were waiting. Troops were sent in but failed to seize the weapons. On the route back to Dublin a crowd began to jeer at the soldiers, who eventually opened fire. Three people were killed and thirty-eight wounded. Nationalists were very angry at this and felt that the authorities were much harder on nationalist gunrunners than on unionists.

Source K
Unionist propaganda designed to win support from the English.

● *List the dangers shown in the picture which the unionists feared.*

Source L
Irish National Volunteers in civilian clothes drilling with guns landed at Howth.

A possible solution – partition

By 1914, it was clear that the Liberals' determination to impose Home Rule on the Ulster unionists was weakening. The government tried to negotiate with both sides and failed to please either. There were two opposing private armies marching and drilling in Ireland.

The unionist proposal that all, or part, of Ulster should be left out of the Home Rule plans became a possibility. The term 'partition' began to be used. John Redmond tried to reassure the Liberals that Ulster Protestant religion and culture would be respected and protected by Dublin, and nationalists protested that the whole island of Ireland was one natural unit, which should not be divided.

These protests were largely unsuccessful. The discussion in Parliament now was not on whether Ulster could opt out, but about what form this opt-out should take, how many counties would be involved and what powers an Ulster assembly should have. By March 1914 a plan was presented to satisfy the unionists. It was proposed that any county in Ireland could vote to opt out of a Home Rule Parliament for six years. Four counties in north-east Ulster with Protestant majorities – Antrim, Armagh, Down and Londonderry – would vote to be outside Home Rule. The unionists also wanted Fermanagh and Tyrone, and Carson used the slogan 'Ulster will fight, and Ulster will be right' to argue the case for the Six Counties.

The Curragh incident

One factor that made the British government move towards partition was that they were not sure that the army could be relied upon to force Ulster into Home Rule. In March 1914 the government was considering the possibility of a clash between the army and the UVF. Sir Arthur Paget, the soldier in charge of the army in Ireland, spoke to army officers in the main camp at the Curragh, near Dublin. Some of them said that they would resign rather than fight against the UVF.

The Buckingham Palace conference

By July 1914 it seemed that Ireland was on the verge of a civil war. The nationalists and the unionists both had armed forces. The British army was unlikely to take sides. The situation was so serious that the King, George V, intervened to try to help. Unionist and nationalist representatives met at Buckingham Palace for private talks on how to avoid violence.

The talks failed and an armed struggle between the UVF and the Irish Volunteers seemed inevitable.

Source M

This *Punch* cartoon shows John Bull, representing Britain, trying to persuade Carson and Redmond to co-operate with each other to secure peace for Ireland.

War is declared

The British Prime Minister, Asquith, seemed to have lost control of the situation in Ireland and the danger of civil war drifted closer and closer. Developments in Europe changed all this. In August 1914 German troops invaded Belgium. In response, Britain declared war on Germany. The UVF were ordered by Carson to help the British war effort. John Redmond said that Irish Volunteers would fight for 'little Catholic Belgium'. Both leaders urged their followers to join the British army in order to fight against the Germans and to show their loyalty to Britain.

At Westminster the main political parties set aside most of their disagreements to lead a united country in the war against Germany. In September 1914 Asquith told MPs that the Home Rule Bill would be made law, but that it would not be put into effect until the war was over – this was at a time when most people thought the fighting would be over by Christmas. The Prime Minister did add, however, that special arrangements would be made for Ulster.

Source P

A recruiting poster encouraging Irish men to join the British army during the First World War.

Source N

Redmond spoke in the House of Commons as soon as war was declared.

I say to the Government that they may tomorrow withdraw every one of their troops from Ireland. The armed Catholics in the South will only be too glad to join arms with the armed Protestant Ulstermen.

Source O

Carson sent this telegram to the UVF leadership when war broke out. He wanted members to join the British army to fight against Germany.

All officers, non-commissioned officers and men who are in the Ulster Volunteer Force are requested to answer immediately His Majesty's call, as our first duty as loyal subjects is to the King.

---

1 Make a list of the ways in which unionists demonstrated their opposition to Home Rule between 1906 and 1914.

2 In what ways did the nationalists copy the actions of the unionists?

3 Compare the Larne and Howth gunrunning episodes.
a How were they similar?
b How were they different?

4 a Describe in your own words the meaning of partition.
b Suggest reasons why partition was being considered as a possible solution to the crisis.

5 What effect did the outbreak of war have on the Home Rule crisis in Ireland in 1914?

Rebellion and partition

1 Thousands of Catholic and Protestant Irish men fought in the First World War. The war dragged on for four years and huge numbers were killed and wounded. Casualties among Ulster Protestants were particularly heavy during the Battle of the Somme in 1916.

2 A small group of nationalists saw the war as an opportunity to rebel against British power. The rebellion took place at Easter 1916. It was led by Patrick Pearse. The rebels took control of central Dublin before they were defeated by the British army. At first most Irish people disapproved of the Easter Rising.

3 Leading figures in the Easter Rising were executed by the British without a proper trial. Many Irish people were sickened by the executions. This increased respect and admiration for the rebels.

4 After the Easter Rising, nationalists began to support Sinn Féin instead of the Irish Parliamentary Party. Sinn Féin won most of the Irish seats in the 1918 General Election. The Sinn Féin MPs set up their own parliament in Dublin, called Dáil Éireann.

5 Survivors of the Easter Rising organised a new campaign of violence between 1919 and 1921. They were now known as the Irish Republican Army. The British used tough methods to try to beat the IRA. In these two years over 1,500 people were killed. Six counties in the north were divided from the rest of Ireland in 1920 and became the new state of Northern Ireland. There was much violence between Catholics and Protestants in the north.

6 Some of the IRA and Sinn Féin leaders, including Michael Collins (above), made a deal with the British Prime Minister, Lloyd George in 1921. An independent state, known as the Irish Free State, was set up in southern Ireland. Some IRA members were angry at this deal and there was a civil war in the Free State from 1922 to 1923.

13

Ireland and the First World War

The outbreak of war in 1914 had an enormous impact on Irish politics. Many unionists and nationalists stopped their campaigning and supported the British war effort.

Why did men on both sides join the British army?

Unionists

The war was an opportunity for Ulster Protestants to show their patriotism. In return, they expected the British government to allow most of Ulster to remain outside of the Home Rule arrangements for Ireland when the war was finally over. The British military leader, Lord Kitchener, was glad to have Ulster Protestants in the army but he wanted them to join existing regiments. Carson disagreed. He wanted the Protestant Ulstermen to be kept together, organised like the UVF. This would be good publicity for the unionist cause. Eventually Kitchener gave way. He had hoped to gain a brigade (about 3,000 men) from Ulster, but Carson promised him a division, (three brigades). Carson kept his promise and so the 36th (Ulster) Division was created.

Source A

I say to you, account yourselves as men in defence of right, of freedom and of religion in this war.

John Redmond speaking to the Irish Volunteers, September 1914

Nationalists

John Redmond encouraged Irish nationalists to join the British army. For leaders of the Irish Party the war seemed like a good opportunity to show that they were supporters of the British Empire – just like people in Canada and Australia who had their own Parliament but kept strong links with Britain. Like the unionists, the leaders expected gratitude from the British at the end of the war.

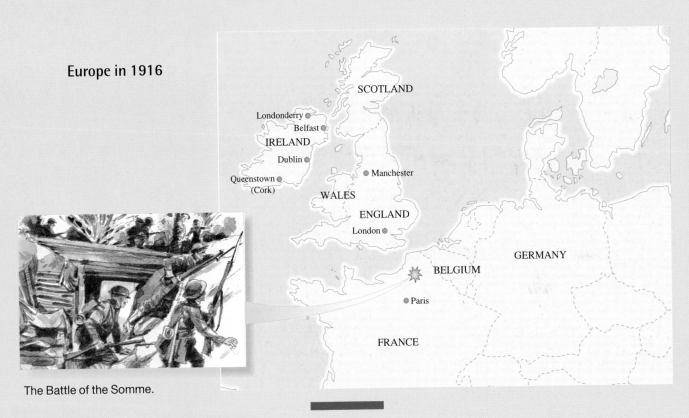

Europe in 1916

The Battle of the Somme.

John Redmond also argued that Belgium was a small Catholic country which had been invaded and Ireland, another small country, should help. Redmond, like Carson, wanted his men to be allowed to form an army unit of their own. However, the British government were not prepared to set up a nationalist division. Redmond's men had to join the existing Irish regiments in the British army and many of them joined the 16th (Irish) Division. In September 1914 the British government suspended the introduction of the Home Rule Act until after the end of the war. The Prime Minister, Asquith, promised the unionists that after the war special arrangements would be made for much of Ulster. At the time, the war was not expected to last long. Certainly no one could foresee the four long years that would pass and the millions of lives that would be lost.

Source C

Both of these extracts are taken from *Sacrifice on the Somme*. Jack Campbell came from a poor family in Dublin, and joined the Royal Army Medical Corps. Jack Christie came from a poor Protestant family in Belfast, and joined the 36th (Ulster) Division.

> The eldest brother was always on about seeing the world. Well, we weren't financially in a position to go to see the world. He figured out that by joining the army you could see the world.
>
> Jack Campbell

> It wasn't a challenge or anything to do with patriotism, it was simply, here's an escape route to get out of the mill, for surely life holds more than this mill can offer.
>
> Jack Christie

Source B

The Royal Irish Rifles on the Somme.

Never before had so many soldiers from so many nations gone into battle at one time. After a few weeks the rapid movement of armies stopped and, for the next four years, millions of men fought in hundreds of miles of trenches dug across the European countryside. Again and again troops with rifles and bayonets fixed were ordered out of their trenches to attempt a breakthrough, only to become entangled in barbed wire and to be slaughtered by artillery shells and machine-gun fire.

Around 170,000 Irish men, nationalists and unionists, Catholics and Protestants, volunteered to join regiments in the British army. In August 1914 the Royal Munster Fusiliers were almost wiped out in the Battle of Mons in Belgium. The 10th Irish Division lost over 5,000 men on the Gallipoli peninsula. On 8 May 1915 the volunteers of the Ulster Division marched through the centre of Belfast before leaving for France. They were being trained to take part in the biggest battle the world had yet seen: the Somme.

Opposition to the war

A minority of Irish people opposed the war. What were the motives of those who objected to the war?

Fenians and Sinn Féin

To the small group of Fenians the idea of joining the British army was unthinkable. A few of the more radical Irish Volunteers, about 11,000, refused to join the army and this caused a split. The great majority, who remained loyal to Redmond, became known as the National Volunteers, and the minority retained the name of Irish Volunteers.

Source D

Arthur Griffith of Sinn Féin was also opposed to Irishmen fighting in the war.

> Ireland is not at war with Germany. England is at war with Germany. Our duty is in no doubt. We are Irish Nationalists and the only duty we have is to stand for Ireland's interests.

Connolly and the socialists

James Connolly and his socialist Irish Citizen Army were completely against the war. They thought that working people from all countries should be comrades and unite to fight their common enemy, the wealthy capitalists. However, this was not a popular view. The British Labour Party and the German Democratic Socialists did not oppose the war.

The Somme, 1916

At the beginning of July 1916 the 36th Ulster Division suffered over 5,500 casualties. Of these, about 2,000 died in just two days of fighting during the Battle of the Somme. The Somme attack was planned to break through the German defences and lead to victory. The British believed that a massive artillery bombardment would destroy the German defences so that infantry could capture the German trenches with little opposition. When the attack began on 1 July 1916, the Germans were waiting and their machine guns cut down wave after wave of British troops. The 36th Ulster Division managed to capture their objective but were exposed to German cross-fire and suffered very heavy casualties. Many Ulstermen were decorated for bravery, four of them receiving the highest award – the Victoria Cross. It was the extent of the loss and the effect on the Ulster communities that made the Somme a key event in Irish history.

Source E
The Charge of the Ulster Division at the Battle of the Somme, James Beadle RA.

Source F

The Ulster Division has lost very heavily, and in doing so has sacrificed itself for the Empire. The Ulster Volunteer Force, from whom the Division was made, has won a name which equals any in history. Their devotion deserves the gratitude of the British Empire.

The Times, 7 July 1916

Source G

A historian's view of the Somme:

When the majority of Ireland became the Free State in 1921, most of Ulster was not forced into the unwanted union with the Catholic South. The sacrifice by the men of the Ulster Division in the war was a factor in influencing this concession.

M. Middlebrook, *The First Day of the Somme,* 1971

Source H

A historian's view of the importance of the war:

The First World War should be seen as one of the most decisive events in modern Irish history. It temporarily defused the Ulster situation; it put Home Rule on ice, it altered the military crisis in Ireland and it created the scene for IRB rebellion in 1916.

R. Foster, *Modern Ireland,* 1989

Source I

A poster advertising the Somme Heritage Centre.
• *How do centres like this help us to understand events in the past?*

AN EXPERIENCE TO REMEMBER

Travel back in time and relive the Battle of the Somme. As you walk along the trenches, look into No Man's Land and experience the sights and sounds of the battlefield.

SOMME HERITAGE CENTRE

OPEN	April - September:	Tuesday - Saturday 10 am - 6pm
		Sunday - 11am - 6pm
	October - March:	Tuesday - Saturday 10am - 5pm
		Sunday 11am - 5pm

(open Mondays in July and August, and all Bank Holiday Mondays)

For further information contact :
Somme Heritage Centre, Bangor Road, Newtownards, Co. Down. Tel: (0247) 823202

---

1 Complete the grid explaining why the nationalist and unionist leaders urged their supporters to join the British army in 1914.

	Redmond	Carson
Reason for joining the British army		
What they hoped to gain at the end of the war		

2 Look at Source C (Christie and Campbell). What reason does each man have for joining the army? Do they share the same reasons as Carson or Redmond?

3 Which Irish people were opposed to the war? Explain why.

4 What were the results of the Ulster Division's sacrifice at the Somme?

5 Look at Sources G and H. What important effects did the First World War have on events in Irish history?

14

The Easter Rising

Irish politics took a surprising turn in 1916. A group of republicans organised a rebellion against British rule. For a week the rebels fought for control of central Dublin.

What happened during the Easter Rising? How did people react to the rebellion?

Source A

The following source describes the British view of the mood in Ireland in 1916.

The general state of Ireland is thoroughly satisfactory. The mass of the people are sound and loyal as regards war and the country is in a very prosperous state and free from ordinary crime.

Major Ivor Price, Director of Military Intelligence in Ireland, in a report dated 10 April 1916

The great majority of people living in Ireland in 1916 would have agreed with Major Price's report. They still supported the war effort; many people, both Catholic and Protestant, were in France fighting for the Empire. Ireland seemed contented and peaceful. There was no danger of invasion. Farmers got good prices for their meat, eggs and butter. There was no shortage of work in the linen and woollen mills where uniforms, blankets, kit bags and material for aircraft wings were made. So many ships were sunk by U-boats that 30,000 men worked in Belfast shipyards in an effort to replace them. While a terrible conflict raged on the European mainland, Ireland was less disturbed than anyone could remember.

The leaders of the uprising

There were, however, small groups in Ireland, who believed Henry Grattan's statement made during the American War of Independence in the 18th century: 'England's difficulty is Ireland's opportunity.' Soon after the beginning of the war, revolutionary nationalists began to plan a rising against British rule.

Tom Clarke ▶
(born in 1857)
Clarke was a Fenian who had served a 15-year prison term for his involvement in dynamite attacks on police stations in the 1880s.

Sean MacDermott ▶
(born in 1884)
MacDermott was a member of the Gaelic League, Sinn Féin and the Gaelic Athletic Association. He was the secretary of the IRB.

Padraic Pearse ▶
(born in 1879)
Pearse was a
writer and
teacher. He had
been a member
of the IRB since
1913.

James Connolly (born in 1868) ▼
Connolly was a labour activist and socialist
thinker. He was a founder of the Irish Citizen
Army.

Thomas MacDonagh (born in 1878) ▶
MacDonagh was a poet, teacher and
Gaelic League member.

◀ **Eamonn Ceannt (born in 1881)**
Ceannt was a prominent member
of the Gaelic League and a
musician.

Joseph Plunkett (born in 1887) ▲
Plunkett was a writer, poet and one of
the founders of the Irish Volunteeers.

Planning the uprising

Most of the nationalist volunteers, like the Ulster Volunteers, supported Britain during the war. A minority, led by Eoin MacNeill and numbering around 11,000, refused to fight with the British armed forces in France. A small number of these Irish Volunteers were involved in planning the rebellion. They were members of the secret Irish Republican Brotherhood (IRB). James Connolly agreed to support the IRB insurrection with his Irish Citizen Army which had been formed to protect striking workers from the police in 1913. Although most of the people who took part in the Easter Rising were men, the women's organisation, Cumann na mBan, was also involved. The best known woman who took part in the rising was Countess Markievicz. She was the daughter of a wealthy landowner in County Sligo who had married a Polish count.

The rising was planned to take place on Easter Sunday, 23 April 1916. But the plans were disrupted by the loss of a shipment of arms from Germany being brought to Ireland by Sir Roger Casement. On Good Friday a German vessel, the Aud, was captured off the coast of County Kerry by the Royal Navy and soon after was scuttled in Cork Harbour with the loss of 20,000 rifles for the IRB. Casement landed by U-boat at Banna Strand in County Kerry, where he was recognised and arrested. The capture of Casement and

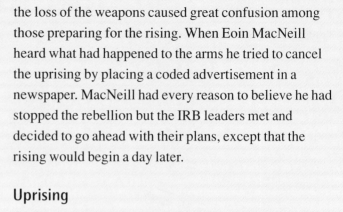

Source B
Countess Markievicz (1868 – 1927).

the loss of the weapons caused great confusion among those preparing for the rising. When Eoin MacNeill heard what had happened to the arms he tried to cancel the uprising by placing a coded advertisement in a newspaper. MacNeill had every reason to believe he had stopped the rebellion but the IRB leaders met and decided to go ahead with their plans, except that the rising would begin a day later.

Uprising

On Easter Monday insurgents occupied important buildings in the centre of Dublin including the General Post Office which had been chosen as the headquarters of the rising. With socialist and republican flags flying in the centre of the city, Pearse stood on the pavement outside the GPO to read the Proclamation of the Republic to a bewildered crowd of Dubliners who were enjoying the Bank Holiday.

Source C
The Proclamation declaring the establishment of an Irish Republic.

POBLACHT NA H EIREANN.
THE PROVISIONAL GOVERNMENT
OF THE
IRISH REPUBLIC
TO THE PEOPLE OF IRELAND.

IRISHMEN AND IRISHWOMEN : In the name of God and of the dead generations from which she receives her old tradition of nationhood, Ireland, through us, summons her children to her flag and strikes for her freedom.

Having organised and trained her manhood through her secret revolutionary organisation, the Irish Republican Brotherhood, and through her open military organisations, the Irish Volunteers and the Irish Citizen Army, having patiently perfected her discipline, having resolutely waited for the right moment to reveal itself, she now seizes that moment, and, supported by her exiled children in America and by gallant allies in Europe, but relying in the first on her own strength, she strikes in full confidence of victory.

We declare the right of the people of Ireland to the ownership of Ireland, and to the unfettered control of Irish destinies, to be sovereign and indefeasible. The long usurpation of that right by a foreign people and government has not extinguished the right, nor can it ever be extinguished except by the destruction of the Irish people. In every generation the Irish people have asserted their right to national freedom and sovereignty; six times during the past three hundred years they have asserted it in arms. Standing on that fundamental right and again asserting it in arms in the face of the world, we hereby proclaim the Irish Republic as a Sovereign Independent State, and we pledge our lives and the lives of our comrades-in-arms to the cause of its freedom, of its welfare, and of its exaltation among the nations.

The Irish Republic is entitled to, and hereby claims, the allegiance of every Irishman and Irishwoman. The Republic guarantees religious and civil liberty, equal rights and equal opportunities to all its citizens, and declares its resolve to pursue the happiness and prosperity of the whole nation and of all its parts, cherishing all the children of the nation equally, and oblivious of the differences carefully fostered by an alien government, which have divided a minority from the majority in the past.

Until our arms have brought the opportune moment for the establishment of a permanent National Government, representative of the whole people of Ireland and elected by the suffrages of all her men and women, the Provisional Government, hereby constituted, will administer the civil and military affairs of the Republic in trust for the people.

We place the cause of the Irish Republic under the protection of the Most High God, Whose blessing we invoke upon our arms, and we pray that no one who serves that cause will dishonour it by cowardice, inhumanity, or rapine. In this supreme hour the Irish nation must, by its valour and discipline and by the readiness of its children to sacrifice themselves for the common good, prove itself worthy of the august destiny to which it is called.

Signed on behalf of the Provisional Government,
THOMAS J. CLARKE,
SEAN Mac DIARMADA, THOMAS MacDONAGH.
P. H. PEARSE, EAMONN CEANNT,
JAMES CONNOLLY. JOSEPH PLUNKETT.

The GPO was open for business and two soldiers who happened to be buying stamps became the first 'prisoners of war'. Any policemen or soldiers who resisted the rebels were shot. The rebels failed to capture Dublin Castle and the telephone exchange so government organisation and communications were still in place.

Dublin during the rising

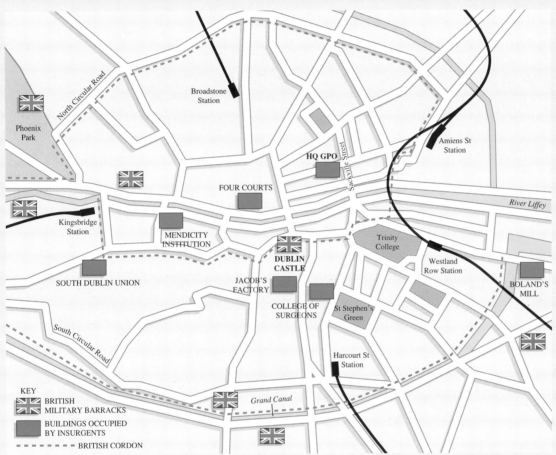

The insurgents had taken everybody by surprise on Easter Monday, but they numbered fewer than 2,000. The odds soon built up against them. Troops were brought in from the Curragh on Monday evening and on Tuesday soldiers who had been destined to fight in France began to land at Kingstown (Dun Laoghaire) six miles south of Dublin. The insurgents held the GPO, the Royal College of Surgeons, the Four Courts, Boland's Mills, the South Dublin Union and several other buildings in the city centre; but they were pinned down by machine-gun fire from the Shelbourne Hotel and from nearby barracks which were occupied by government troops.

On the afternoon of Wednesday 26 April a column of British troops, marching into the city from Kingstown, were ambushed by twelve volunteers. More than 200 British soldiers were killed. The gunboat *Helga* sailed up the Liffey and fired shells at buildings held by the insurgents. The people of Dublin did not join the rising. Instead poor people looted the shops.

On Thursday, guns in Trinity College shelled O'Connell Street and by Friday afternoon the GPO was on fire. After bitter street fighting, the rebels realised they were beaten. At 2.30 pm on Saturday 29 April, Pearse and Connolly signed an unconditional surrender and they and their men were led away by British troops.

Source D

British troops behind a barricade, during the Rising.

Source E

Brighid Lyons Thornton, a young girl at that time who helped to carry messages and make food for the rebels, described what happened:

We were all lined up in the barracks square and one of the first in the rank we joined was the Countess Markievicz, in her green turned-up hat and her put-tees and breeches and her tunic. Now we never had the British to protect us before, but luckily this time the soldiers guarded us very heavily because when the gates were opened and we were marched out there were such shrieks of hatred. Never did I see such savage women. A lot of them were getting the separation allowance because their husbands were off fighting in France and they thought their livelihood would be taken away because of what we had done. A lot of it seemed to be directed against the Countess's breeches and puttees.

Quoted in *Curious Journey,* 1982

This modern illustration shows the scene inside the GPO before the surrender.

1 Explain why (a) Padraic Pearse and (b) James Connolly planned a rebellion at Easter 1916.

2 Why did Eoin MacNeill try to cancel the rising?

3 Why were people bewildered at the sight of the rebels at the GPO?

4 Look at Source E (Brighid Thornton). Why did the women of Dublin react so strongly to the captured rebels?

5 Write a brief newspaper report telling the story of Easter Week from Monday to Saturday.

15

Reactions to the Rising

There was little popular support for the Easter Rising at the time. A great change took place in people's attitudes after it had failed.

What effect did the Easter Rising and its aftermath have on people's attitudes in Ireland?

The executions

The British commanding officer in Ireland was General Sir John Maxwell. He was a strong supporter of the British Empire. He thought that the rebellion had been a disgraceful event. Maxwell believed that by severely punishing the rebels he would prevent further trouble.

Maxwell ignored advice of this kind. Within days of the rebellion he began to execute some of the participants by firing squad. They were not given a proper trial. Pearse and two others were shot on 3 May. During the next few days a total of fifteen men were shot. As the shootings continued, many people in Ireland became sickened by the executions.

On 12 May Connolly was shot, bringing the executions to an end. However, other harsh penalties continued. MacNeill, who had tried, with some success, to stop the Rising, was sentenced to life imprisonment. A total of 3,500 people were arrested and held without trial, many of whom had no connection with the rebellion. Nearly 2,000 people were transported to prisons and camps in Britain. Casement was tried for treason and hanged in London. The mood in Ireland was changing. People began to speak of the rebels with respect and admiration.

Source A

John Dillon was the deputy leader of the Irish Parliamentary Party. He wrote to his leader, Redmond, from his home close to the GPO immediately after the end of the rebellion:

> The wisest course is to execute no one for the present. If there were shootings of prisoners on a large scale the effect on public opinion might be disastrous in the extreme.

Source B

While the executions were still going on, Dillon argued for moderation in this speech to the House of Commons on 11 May:

> It is not murderers who are being executed; it is insurgents who have fought a clean fight. You are washing out our whole life's work in a sea of blood. Thousands of people, who ten days ago were bitterly opposed to the whole Sinn Féin movement and to the rebellion, are now becoming infuriated against the government on account of these executions.

Source C

Another member of the Irish Party also noticed the changing mood.

> I never knew such a transformation of opinion as that caused by the executions. They have lost the hearts of the people beyond all hope of retrieving their mistakes.

Tim Healy, 10 June 1916

KILMAINHAM MAY 1916

Source D

An unsigned painting of one of the executions in Kilmainham Jail, May 1916.

Source F

A modern historian's view:

> The Easter Rising was a watershed, changing the political situation in Ireland. From the start of the World War there had been growing discontent with Redmond's party but now the Rising and the ferocity of the British response led to a tide of sympathy for the rebels.

Liz Curtis, *The Cause of Ireland*, 1994

Source E

Many thousands of nationalists were in the British army at the time of the Easter Rising. One, who later became a leading member of the IRA, remembered the impact of the news from Dublin.

> In 1916 I was in Mesopotamia [modern Iraq] with the British Expeditionary Force. Outside the orderly room I saw a notice. It told of this rising in Dublin, and the execution of men I'd never heard of and I said to myself, 'What the hell am I doing with the British army? It's with the Irish I should be!'

Tom Barry, quoted in *Curious Journey*, 1982

---

1 Compare the reaction of ordinary Dubliners to the Rising with their later reaction to the executions.

2 With a partner, choose the role of either General Maxwell or John Dillon. Write a short speech giving your chosen personality's views on how the Easter rebels should be treated.

16

The rise of Sinn Féin and the first Dáil Éireann

Before the First World War, Sinn Féin had been a small, insignificant organisation. In the election held in 1918 Sinn Féin became the biggest single political party in Ireland.

What were the consequences of this victory for Sinn Féin?

The Easter Rising had been organised by the secret Irish Republican Brotherhood. Few people had heard of the IRB and they mistakenly thought that Sinn Féin had been behind the rebellion. Sinn Féin in fact played no part in the Easter Rising but afterwards the survivors used Sinn Féin as their political party.

Redmond and the Irish Parliamentary Party became concerned that nationalists would stop supporting them and switch to Sinn Féin. They wanted the British government to introduce Home Rule immediately in order to end the crisis. In May and June 1916 the British politician, Lloyd George, tried to arrange a deal on Home Rule involving the exclusion of six Ulster counties. Nationalists and unionists argued about whether the exclusion was permanent or temporary and the plan collapsed.

Most of the rebel prisoners were kept in a camp in Wales at a place called Frongoch, and some started to plan another uprising. A new leader, called Michael Collins, emerged. He had taken an active part in the Rising and had been at the GPO with Pearse and Connolly. While he admired the bravery of the dead men, he questioned the tactics of the leaders of the Rising and began to think about more effective ways of using violence against the British forces. By December 1916 Lloyd George had become the British Prime Minister and he released hundreds of the prisoners from Frongoch including Collins.

Sinn Féin did not have much success in elections before the Easter Rising. This began to change in

1917. Sinn Féin was seen as the party of the rebels and it began to grow in popularity. Slowly it came to replace the Irish Parliamentary Party as the main political party in Ireland. Eamon de Valera, who had taken part in the Easter Rising, became the president of Sinn Féin. In 1917 he won an important victory in a by-election in East Clare.

Source A

This banner belonged to a Sinn Féin branch named after Eamon de Valera.

70

Conscription

By 1918 there had been a serious fall in the number of volunteers for the armed services. The government therefore decided to introduce conscription in Ireland: Irish men could be forced by law to join the armed forces. After the events of 1916 and the treatment of the rebels, this caused uproar in Ireland.

As a protest the Irish Parliamentary Party withdrew from Parliament and returned to Ireland. The annual meeting of the Catholic bishops issued a statement condemning conscription in Ireland. Representatives of a number of groups drafted a 'National Pledge' against conscription, copies of which were signed by huge numbers of people on 21 April. The trade unions called a one-day strike in protest. The Women Workers' Union marched through Dublin and vowed to support the men in their resistance. The protests persuaded the British not to introduce conscription in Ireland.

The government then announced that there was a 'German plot' and imprisoned more republicans. All this helped Sinn Féin to gain more support at the expense of the Irish Parliamentary Party.

On 11 November 1918 the First World War ended and in December 1918 a General Election was held. There had been no election since 1910 and for the first time every adult male could vote and some women as well; the Irish electorate was increased almost three times in size. Sinn Féin won 73 out of a total of 107 seats; the Irish Parliamentary Party was reduced to 6 seats, only one of them outside Ulster; the Unionists increased from 18 to 26 seats; and, in Britain, the Conservatives – most of them strongly opposed to Sinn Féin – won more than half the seats in the House of Commons. A struggle between Irish republicans and the government of the British Empire was certain.

The Dáil

Having swept away much of the Irish Party in the General Election, the victorious Sinn Féin MPs refused to go to the London Parliament. Instead they set up their own Parliament in Dublin. They met together for the first time in Dublin in January 1919 and the Parliament was called Dáil Éireann.

Source B
This modern painting by Tom Ryan shows The Dáil in session.

> **1** Why were Irishmen opposed to conscription in 1918?
>
> **2 a** Give two reasons why Sinn Féin was successful in the General Election of 1918.
> **b** Which do you think was the most important reason and why?

17

The War of Independence

On the same day as the Dáil Éireann met for the first time in January 1919, two policemen were shot dead in Soloheadbeg, County Tipperary. This was the start of a war of independence fought by an organisation called the Irish Republican Army.

What happened during this violent period of Irish history?

In order to gain a completely independent Ireland, some republicans renewed the military conflict with the British forces that had started in Easter Week 1916. The IRA claimed to be the army of the new independent Ireland set up by Dáil Éireann. Between 1919 and 1921 the IRA fought a bitter guerrilla war against the British army and the police. Led by Michael Collins, the IRA concentrated on secret arson attacks and ambushes of the British forces.

The Black and Tans

The British Prime Minister, Lloyd George, sent reinforcements from Britain to help the Irish police. These reinforcements were mostly unemployed British ex-servicemen. They wore a makeshift uniform – a mixture of police black and army khaki – and they soon became known as the 'Black and Tans'. Together with new recruits called Auxiliaries – former officers from the British army – the Black and Tans soon gained a reputation for brutality. When the IRA attacked and killed police, the Black and Tans were likely to burn houses and shoot suspects as a reprisal. These reprisals had the effect of greatly strengthening nationalist support for the IRA.

Source A

The British Labour Party produced a report in 1920 that condemned the Black and Tans. The report made the point that the reprisals greatly strengthened support for the IRA and Sinn Féin.

The IRA are fed and harboured by people who three years ago were certainly not Sinn Féiners and some of whom were Unionists. So great has been the provocation from the British government that 80 per cent of Irish men and women now regard the shooting of policemen and the throwing of bombs with resignation. Under such conditions it is practically impossible to keep the Irish Republican Army at bay.

Source B

A group of Black and Tans.

Despite many protests Lloyd George allowed the policy of Black and Tan reprisals to continue and the violence increased. For most of 1920 a bitter guerrilla war raged over much of Ireland, especially in Munster and around Dublin. The IRA continued to attack police barracks, lay ambushes for police patrols and kill those thought to be helping the government. No more than a few thousand fought with the IRA but they had support from many who had voted for Sinn Féin.

Source C

Men of the South, a picture of an IRA flying column, painted by Sean Keating.

● *Do you think this is a realistic image of a flying column? Give reasons for your answer.*

In 1920 the IRA began to form 'flying squads' of several dozen men to carry out ambushes and attacks. On the morning of Sunday 21 November 1920, men in an IRA squad, under orders from Michael Collins, murdered fourteen British officers believed to be undercover agents. That afternoon, in an act of revenge, the Black and Tans shot dead twelve spectators and one Gaelic football player at Croke Park in Dublin and wounded sixty others. That night three IRA prisoners were murdered by Auxiliaries in the guardroom of Dublin Castle. People remembered that day as 'Bloody Sunday'.

A week after Bloody Sunday a flying column led by Tom Barry ambushed a motor convoy at Kilmichael in west Cork: seventeen Auxiliaries were killed. Two weeks later Auxiliaries, in retaliation, set fire to parts of Cork city centre causing damage estimated at £3 million. In 1921 the British government began to use the British army,

which was much more successful against the IRA. On 25 May the IRA suffered a disastrous defeat. The Dublin Custom House, the centre of nine government departments, was attacked by about 120 IRA men and set on fire. Troops and police quickly surrounded and captured most of them and took nearly all their weapons. De Valera, seeing how weak the IRA now was, began to explore ways of ending the fighting. The British government was winning the war against the IRA in 1921 but Lloyd George faced growing criticism in Britain and from his allies for the methods he was using. Even while the war of independence raged, the British government was trying to find a new political solution to the Irish problem.

---

1 Look at Source A (Labour Party Report 1920). What reasons can you find to explain support for the IRA?

2 Why did Lloyd George and de Valera decide to try to find a political solution to the problems in Ireland?

18

Dividing Ireland

While the IRA was fighting the war of independence, the British government had set up a committee to try to solve the Ulster problem. This committee recommended dividing Ireland into two parts: Northern Ireland and the Irish Free State.

What were the effects of the partition of Ireland?

The Government of Ireland Act was passed in 1920. It separated six of the nine counties of Ulster from the rest of Ireland, and set up two Parliaments: one in Dublin and one in Belfast. The original proposal had been to separate nine counties, including Donegal, Monaghan and Cavan, from the rest of Ireland. Because of the large number of Catholics living in these three counties, the unionists were afraid that their majority would be too small. They preferred the option of the six counties where their majority was safe.

Northern Ireland after the partition

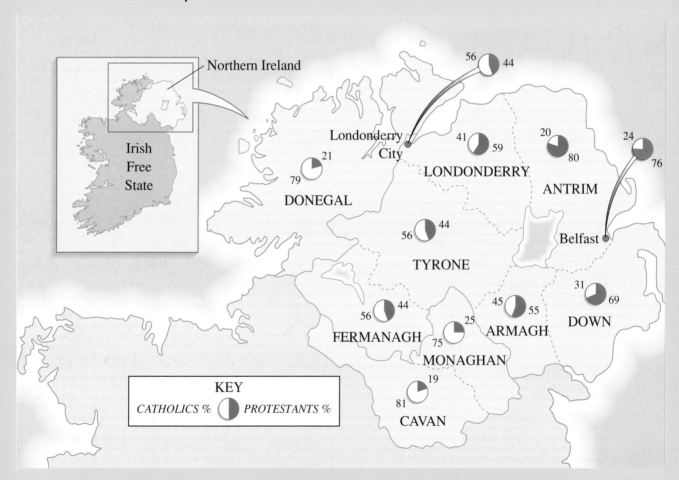

The symbols on each county show the proportion of Catholics to Protestants.

The British government gave the unionists what they wanted: Northern Ireland would be in the United Kingdom; the six-county area would have a large Protestant majority; and unionists would be certain to control the Parliament in Belfast. The IRA and Sinn Féin leaders did not want partition and now they wanted to go further than Home Rule – their call was for a completely independent republic.

As unionists and nationalists opposed each other over partition, so the underlying sectarian conflicts and fears became more apparent. Bitter fighting broke out in Ulster between Catholics and Protestants. The IRA actively and violently attempted to disrupt the new state of Northern Ireland. The Ulster Volunteer Force was set up again in June 1920. During clashes between the IRA and the UVF in Londonderry, eight Catholics and four Protestants were killed. The British army moved in but the shooting and the killing went on. During the summer of 1920 violence spread to Belfast. The government formed a Special Constabulary to fight the IRA in Ulster. Many of the UVF joined the new police force. Catholics were not encouraged to join the Special Constabulary and most of the 'Specials' were Protestants. The IRA threatened to kill anyone who joined the Specials.

Source A

One Catholic later recalled the attack on the nationalist workers in the Belfast shipyards.

The gates were smashed down with sledges, the vests and shirts of those at work were torn open to see if the men were wearing any Catholic emblems, and woe betide the man who was. One man was set upon, thrown into the dock, had to swim the Musgrave Channel, and having been pelted with rivets, had to swim two or three miles, to emerge in streams of blood and rush to the police office in a nude state.

Quoted in M. Farrell, *The Orange State,* 1976.

In Northern Ireland Sinn Féin and the nationalists decided that, if elected, they would refuse to take their seats in the Belfast Parliament as a protest against partition.

In the elections for the Northern Ireland Parliament the Ulster Unionists won forty seats; the Nationalists six seats; and Sinn Féin six seats. Labour did not get any candidate elected.

King George V, in his speech to the Northern Ireland Parliament, had appealed to the people of Ireland to stop the violence. By the middle of 1921 both sides were prepared to listen. After its disastrous attack on the Custom House in Dublin, the IRA had lost too many weapons and too many men. The British army might be able to defeat the IRA but the cost would be too high: governments in other countries would condemn its actions against a people who had voted by a large majority for a republic.

The Treaty

A truce was agreed on 11 July 1921. Eamon de Valera, President of the Dáil, went to London for discussions with Lloyd George, the British Prime Minister. De Valera wanted a 32-county republic and Lloyd George wanted to keep all of Ireland in the British Empire. Formal discussions began in October 1921 but de Valera refused to lead the Irish delegation which was headed by Arthur Griffith and included Michael Collins. Sir James Craig refused an invitation to join the negotiations.

To reach agreement both sides had to compromise. Lloyd George was willing to give the Irish far greater independence than Home Rule. In the end Griffith agreed to let Ireland remain inside the British Empire. The Treaty was signed at 2 am on 6 December 1921: the final concession was that the British government agreed to revise the border between the six and twenty-six counties by setting up a Boundary Commission.

The main points of the Treaty

- Northern Ireland can decide whether to join the Irish Free State.
- If Ireland is to remain divided, a Boundary Commission will decide on possible changes to the border.
- There is to be self-government for the 26 counties – the Irish Free State.
- The Irish Free State is to be part of the British Empire – a dominion like Canada.
- The Free State is to have its own army and police force, but three bases will remain for the use of the Royal Navy.

Source B

This *Punch* cartoon shows Lloyd George as the Welsh Wizard preparing to perform the trick of cutting up Ireland.

Source C

Arthur Griffith (right) and Michael Collins after signing the Treaty in December 1921.

Source D

On the night of the signing of the Treaty, Michael Collins wrote a letter. In this he predicted that the Treaty was not the end of political arguments over Ireland.

> Think, what have I got for Ireland? Something she has wanted these past seven hundred years. Will anyone be satisfied at the bargain? Will anyone? I tell you; early this morning I signed my death warrant.

Source E

Anti-Treaty IRA troops on the streets of Dublin, June 1922.

The Treaty had been signed in London, but would it be accepted in Dublin? De Valera rejected it. There were bitter debates in the Dáil. Many deputies objected to the Irish Free State being in the British Empire – members of the Dáil would have to take an oath of allegiance to the King. Some thought it was wrong that Ireland should be partitioned. Others believed that the Treaty was the best deal that Ireland could get from Britain and that the Irish Free State would in time become a truly independent country. In January 1922 the vote was taken in the Dáil: 64 voted for the Treaty and 57 against. The margin of 7 votes was narrow.

In Northern Ireland violence increased during the first six months of 1922. The Catholics there, one-third of the population, felt they were worse off than when they were ruled directly from London. The IRA was very active and there were vicious sectarian battles between Protestants and Catholics. Only by greatly increasing the numbers of police and by interning suspects did the Northern Ireland government begin to restore order. The violence ended swiftly after the IRA withdrew to take part in the Irish civil war but the problems had not been resolved.

The civil war

Disagreement over the terms of the Treaty left the IRA split down the middle. The anti-Treaty IRA, known as the Irregulars, began to seize weapons, barracks and public buildings. In June 1922 the people of the Irish Free State voted overwhelmingly for the Treaty but civil war between factions supporting and opposing the Treaty broke out at the end of June. In May 1923, after a year of fighting that was in some ways more savage than the war against the British, the Irregulars ended their campaign. By this time Michael Collins had been killed in the fighting and Arthur Griffith had died of a heart attack.

---

1 What were the main terms of the Government of Ireland Act 1920?

2 What compromises did (a) the British government and (b) the nationalist negotiators make in order to reach agreement on the Treaty?

3 What caused the Civil War after the signing of the Treaty?

Conclusion

From partition to the peace process

Northern Ireland and the Irish Free State were born in violence. Even after the anti-Treaty IRA called a halt to the fighting in May 1923, political uncertainty continued. The findings of the Boundary Commission were never published and the border remained the same as it was in 1921.

What happened in Ireland in the years after partition?

In the 1930s, prices for exports of farm produce were low and attempts to set up new industries were not very successful. The great export industries of the North faced growing competition in the world markets. In the 1930s at least a quarter of Northern Ireland's workforce was unemployed.

The Second World War was a very different experience for the two parts of Ireland. The South, renamed Eire in 1937, was neutral. The people there suffered a severe fall in living standards but not the heavy bombing suffered by the North which played a key role in the war against the U-boats.

Source A
Bomb damage to Belfast caused by German air raids.

Eire became a republic in 1949 but the frequent calls made by Dublin governments for an end to partition failed. Greatly improved health, education and other welfare services were introduced in Northern Ireland after the war. The 1960s brought hope as new industries were set up in Ireland – North and South. Nationalists in Northern Ireland campaigned for an end to partition and improved civil rights. Reforms came too late and sectarian hostilities resurfaced. British troops were placed on active service in Northern Ireland when violence erupted in August 1969.

Source B

A British soldier in the centre of Belfast, 1972.

Source C

President Bill Clinton and John Hume of the SDLP acknowledge the cheering crowd at the Guildhall, Derry, during Clinton's visit to Northern Ireland to support the peace process in November 1995.

In the 1970s and 1980s a republican paramilitary group, the Provisional IRA, used bombings and shootings to try to force the British out of Northern Ireland. Loyalist paramilitaries fought to keep the six counties in the United Kingdom. The Northern Ireland government used internment in 1971 but this failed and in 1972 the Westminster government imposed direct rule from London. Many attempts were made to find a political compromise that would satisfy both Protestants and Catholics.

Eventually, both the Provisional IRA and the Combined Loyalist Military Command agreed to separate ceasefires in the late summer of 1994. The negotiations which followed showed that there were no simple solutions to the compli... problems of Northern Ireland.